Rx *for Quilters*

Stitcher–Friendly
Advice for Every Body

SUSAN DELANEY MECH, M.D.

C&T PUBLISHING

Editor: Annie Nelson
Technical Editor: Sara Kate MacFarland
Copyeditor: Vera Tobin
Book Design: Nancy Koerner
Cover Design: Aliza Kahn
Design Director: Diane Pedersen
Graphic Illustrations: Norman Remer
Front Cover: (left to right starting at upper left) Jan Gadberry, Betty Lou Wood, Ginny Kenny and
    Debby Campbell, Bertha Mallard.
Photography: Stephen C. Delaney unless otherwise noted.
Photos on pages 44, 95 and cover image, lower right: Billy Jackson
Photo on page 16: Sharon Risedorph

We take great care to ensure that the information included in this book is accurate and presented in
good faith, but no warranty is provided nor results guaranteed. Since we have no control over your
current medical condition, neither the author nor C&T Publishing, Inc. shall have any liability to any
person or entity with respect to any loss or damage caused directly or indirectly by the information
contained in this book. This book is written as if you, the reader, are a right-handed woman. This is
done for readability and because the author's expertise lies in the area of women's health. If you are
left-handed or a man, or both, she will rely on your forbearance.

**Disclaimer: The information and recommendations presented in this book are based on a care-
ful review of the current medical literature and on the author's 20 years experience as a medical
doctor. This book is not intended to replace sound medical advice from your personal physician.
This is especially important in matters concerning back and neck disorders and pregnancy. No
one should begin an exercise program without consulting her personal physician.**

Library of Congress Cataloging-in Publication Data
Mech, Susan Delaney, 1948–
   Rx for quilters : stitcher-friendly advice for every body /
Susan Delaney Mech.
      p.   cm.
   Includes bibliographical references (p. 111) and index.
   ISBN 1-57120-092-4 (pbk.)
   1. Quilters--Health and hygiene. 2. Quilting--Health aspects. I Title.
   RC965.T4 M435 2000
   613'.024'746--dc21   99-6696
                                       CIP

Trademarked (™) and Registered Trademarked (®) names are used throughout this book. Rather than
use the symbols with every occurrence of a trademark and registered trademark name, we have only
used the symbol the first time the product appears. We are using the names only in an editorial fash-
ion and to the benefit of the owner, with no intention of infringement.

Published by C&T Publishing, Inc.
P.O. Box 1456
Lafayette, California 94549

Printed in China

10   9   8   7   6   5   4   3   2   1

Table of Contents

. . . for the sisterhood of quiltmakers, past, present, and those yet unborn

About the Author

Susan Delaney Mech's love of sewing began as she sat on the floor beside her grandmother's treadle-operated sewing machine. As Susan hand sewed doll clothes while her grandmother used the machine, she found herself wrapped in the same peace and contentment that surrounded her grandmother.

Sewing became one of the constants in Susan's long years of training. Handwork, especially, became her haven from the pressures of school. She graduated from the University of Wisconsin Medical School in 1977.

Susan took up quiltmaking in 1985. She has won many ribbons and special awards for her quilts. In 1988, Susan brought together the love she has for medicine, quiltmaking, and writing and began her long-running column, *Rx for Quilters*, for *Quilt World* magazine.

Susan has published articles on quiltmaking, sewing, and other topics. Her poems have won many awards.

Susan is a nationally-known authority on women's health issues. She has been quoted by the *Ladies' Home Journal*, *Discover* magazine, the Associated Press, and many newspapers. She has published articles in medical journals and has presented many papers and workshops at national meetings. Susan is a member of the American Medical Writers Association.

Introduction

I remember the moment I first took a milliner's needle in hand and sewed together two patches. In that instant I felt my life pivot. My interest in all other crafts fell away. Quilting was what I had been searching for all of my life. In the fifteen years since that day, quilting continues to hold me spellbound. I have begun to understand why.

A simple sewing task, such as sewing together two patches, lowers your heart rate and blood pressure. It sends a wave of relaxation throughout your whole body. This calming is important because of all of the pressures we encounter in our daily lives. We are wives, mothers, caregivers to our aging parents, wage-earners, and volunteers. In the course of our days, we face snarled traffic, new technology, financial pressures, and the challenges of raising children. We need the health and life-giving benefits of quiltmaking.

Quiltmaking offers us the solitude to think our own thoughts, to dream our own dreams, and to plan our lives. Quilting is a constant in our lives that transcends marital state, childbearing, job changes, moves, and losses.

Quiltmaking has calming rhythms that nourish our spirits. The sensual allure of fabric invites us to slow down and enjoy life. When our lives lie in pieces all around us, quiltmaking allows us to create order. Quilting leaves us relaxed, soothed, centered, and aligned.

Quiltmaking involves repetitive movements made over long hours of time. To avoid injury to your hands, wrists, elbows, shoulders, and spine, you must have a healthy respect for the needs and limitations of your body.

When you balance your inner drive to quilt with your body's needs, you can expect to have a lifetime of enjoyable quiltmaking with only minor discomforts.

This book shows you how to care for your body so you can have a comfortable and injury-free quilting life. Watch for the "pennies," which flag money-saving tips.

Every body needs this book. It is my privilege to bring it to you.

Stephanie Tallent (right) has been a quilter for 15 years and is the owner of a long-arm quilting business, Stephanie's Electric Quilts. She is a graduate of Baylor University and is a mom-at-home with Samuel.

Quiltmaking & Your Body

1 Back to Basics— Your Guide to a Comfortable, Pain-free Back

A comfortable, pain-free back is within the reach of most quiltmakers. In this chapter we will explore:
- What backs are like
- The things we quilters do that cause back pain
- What you can do to relieve or eliminate back pain

Your back is a wonderful structure, made up of:
- Bones called vertebrae
- Intervertebral discs that function as spacers and shock absorbers
- Muscles
- Ligaments that function as strapping that binds adjoining bones together

If you want a comfortable, pain-free back, you must understand and respect these structures.

Who Develops Back Pain?

- "Workers who lift heavy objects" make up the largest group of back pain patients
- "Sedentary women," such as quilters, make up the second largest group of back pain patients

If you sit and quilt for hours at a time without a break, you are putting an enormous strain on your back. This chapter helps you find ways to keep your back strong and safe. If you follow the suggestions in this chapter you can probably have a pain-free back. As a wonderful bonus, if you follow these suggestions, *you will also be able to make 25% more quilts in the coming year!*

There are two other risk factors for back pain:
- Being overweight
- Lack of regular exercise

Being overweight increases your risk for back pain because the extra fat in your abdomen stretches and weakens your abdominal muscles. This interferes with an important support for your back. Chapter 13 (page 82) shows you how to design a life-long eating plan that will melt away those extra pounds without ever having to diet again.

Lack of regular exercise weakens both your muscles and your bones, and leaves them vulnerable to injury. Later in this chapter, I will teach you some simple back exercises that you can do in bed, in the shower, and while you are quilting. These easy exercises will help you to stretch and tone your back muscles. They will also strengthen the bones and ligaments of your back. Chapter 14 (page 93) teaches you to "take 10" and go for a short walk whenever you can steal a few minutes from your busy schedule.

A Pain-free Back

Respecting your back's abilities and limitations is the key to having a pain-free back. If you work too hard because of ambition or because of a deadline, you may injure your back. You must balance your drive to create with the limitations of your back itself. This requires a sensible and honest approach to planning your quilts so you have plenty of time to devote to each step of the quiltmaking process. Chapter 12 (page 78) will help you learn to do this.

Sitting and Back Pain

Most of your quiltmaking time will be spent sitting. Sitting puts enormous strain on your back. This is why sedentary women are the second most frequent back pain patients. Your body is designed to engage in a wide variety of activities each hour, including standing, sitting, squatting, and lying down. This variety of movements helps keep your back comfortable and healthy.

Your Bones and Back Pain

Bone is a living tissue that undergoes constant remodeling. Bones that experience unhealthy forces will change their shapes. If you sit for hours each day with your upper back slumped and your head jutting forward, your vertebrae will gradually curve into an uncomfortable and unsightly "dowager's hump." Keep your bones at the peak of health by maintaining good posture.

Your Muscles and Back Pain

Remaining seated for longer than an hour can seriously fatigue the muscles of your back. This causes pain in three ways: the build-up of energy byproducts, prolonged healing time, and muscle spasm. Prevent muscle pain by maintaining good posture and by taking regular stretch and rest breaks.

Your Discs and Back Pain

Sitting flattens your discs. Your discs rely on their rounded shape to do their work. If they flatten, your back nerves can become pinched, resulting in pain. Prevent this pain by taking regular stretch and rest breaks.

Your Ligaments and Back Pain

Sitting for hours without a break can also cause microscopic tears to your back ligaments. These tears are mini-sprains. Prevent these injuries by taking regular stretch and rest breaks.

Fluid Dynamic Posture

Maintaining good posture is a dynamic activity characterized by continuous, tiny movements. Gentle swaying or fidgeting, invisible to anyone else, keeps your muscles, ligaments, and discs in a healthy, pain-free condition. This movement is crucial anytime the upper part of your back is unsupported, as when you sit at the sewing machine or when you quilt at a frame.

IRONING Keep a footstool, six to nine inches high, near your ironing board. Put your left foot on it when you stand to iron. Flexing your hip in this way prevents swayback and forestalls back strain. Almost every surgeon uses a stool such as this while she operates. See page 107 for tips on finding the perfect height for your ironing board.

LIFTING Improper lifting causes many back injuries. Quiltmakers lift heavy boxes of fabric and lug boxes of sewing equipment to workshops and retreats.

Here's how to safely lift a heavy bin of fabric or box by using your knees: Stand close to the bin with your feet planted widely and in line with your shoulders. Bend your knees, tighten your stomach muscles, and grasp the bin firmly. Keep your hips, shoulders, and ears in a straight line. Now lift the bin in one smooth motion by unbending your knees. Hold the bin close to your body and stand as straight as you can. Walk to the drop point and put the bin down by bending your knees. Remember to tighten your stomach muscles and keep your back straight as you unbend your knees.

STANDING Good standing posture begins at the hip. Stand up for a moment and try it.

- Tuck in your tummy. This will flatten your lower spine into a small, graceful curve.
- Tuck in your chin and elongate your neck. Your ear should make a straight line with your shoulder, hip, and ankle.
- Feel the easy balance this posture creates.
- Notice how much less energy it takes to be in good posture.
- Note that you look 5 pounds thinner when you stand in good posture!

LONG-ARM QUILTING Stand with your feet about 12" apart. Keep your head, shoulders, hips, and ankles in a straight line. Excellent lighting facilitates good head posture. Grasp the handles of your machine lightly and remain relaxed as you work. Wear shoes with good arch support while you work. I recommend aerobic shoes because they let you move sideways. See page 106 for tips on setting the height of your machine.

SITTING Seated posture is the most important posture for you to master, because you spend most of your quiltmaking time seated.

- Good seated posture begins with your feet. Keep both feet pressed flat against the floor. This helps you stabilize your hips and lower back.
- Your lower back must have a support of some type. This "lumbar" support may be built into your chair, or you may place a firm cushion or a rolled up towel against the small of your back.
- Your seated posture should resemble your standing posture in that your hip, shoulder, and head form a straight line.

See the photo that introduces this section on page 7.

SLEEP POSTURE Nighttime sleep posture will affect the way your back feels when you quilt. Nighttime is when your body heals the minor injuries that your back sustains every day. When you sleep, keep your head, shoulders, and hips in a straight line, just as you do when sitting:

- Lie on your side with your head on a pillow. The pillow should hold your head off the bed so your head is lined up with your spine. Do not allow your upper shoulder to sag forward and twist your spine. You may need to hug a pillow to prevent this.
- Bend your knees and flex your hips as if you were sitting. Place a firm pillow between your knees to support your upper leg and to keep it from sagging forward and twisting your spine.

Your spine will now be straight. This allows for the healing of any injuries you have sustained during the day and for good blood flow to rinse away all energy breakdown products from the day. Sleeping in good posture will allow your discs to regain their rounded shape.

ROTARY CUTTING Stand with your right foot a little forward of your left. Bend from the waist, keeping your head aligned with your shoulders and hips. Use your whole arm to transmit force to your rotary cutter. Chapter 16 (page 106) offers tips on finding the perfect height for your cutting mat.

WALKING We quiltmakers walk all day when we visit a quilt show. When walking, stride gracefully from the hip, maintaining a straight line from hip to shoulder to head. Swing your arms to help you balance. See page 24 for tips about your shoulder bag. See Chapter 15 (page 100) for tips about attending shows.

POSTURE DURING PREGNANCY Good posture is never more important than in pregnancy. Please see page 54 for tips on the care of your back during pregnancy.

Back Harnesses and Posture

These new devices are controversial. I believe they work against your goal of having strong postural muscles. If you maintain good posture by voluntary effort, you will be strengthening your back every single minute.

If you hang a weight on your back, you will accomplish "good posture" without using your postural muscles. This prevents your postural muscles from getting the workout they need to stay strong. The lack of exercise will weaken them. As they weaken, it will become harder and harder for you to maintain good posture without the weights.

If your postural muscles are weak, begin to do the exercises at the end of this chapter daily. Do them in the morning and during your breaks. In a month's time, you will have strong, healthy postural muscles and you will find it easy to maintain good posture.

Overuse Injuries

Your back needs rest and variety of movement. You *can* have whole days devoted to quiltmaking, but on those days, your quiltmaking tasks must be varied. Stand to iron and then sit to sew. Stand to rotary cut, then sit in your recliner to do some handwork. It is important to have several projects going so you can have diversity in your quilting day.

OVERUSE INJURIES AND ANTI-INFLAMMATORY PAINKILLERS Non-steroidal anti-inflammatory agents such as Motrin® (ibuprofen) or Advil® (naproxen) cause your body to retain water and swell up. Unfortunately, muscles, tendons, and ligaments are more prone to injury when they are swollen.

These drugs also inhibit your white cells and keep them from cleaning up your injured tissues. The cellular debris remains where it falls. Ultimately, this debris hardens into tiny scars, and your muscles, tendons, and ligaments will stiffen and shorten. If you injure your back by overuse, and then take Motrin or Advil for the pain, you can worsen your situation.

Tylenol® (acetaminophen) does not cause swelling or inhibit the white cells, and is better for overuse injury pain; however, it can be toxic in large doses, especially if you use it with alcohol.

Breaks

Your productivity will be increased by 25% if you take a 10-minute break every hour.

The first thing to do during your break is to stretch. Stretching:

- Begins the healing process for the muscles, tendons, or ligaments that are damaged while you work
- Interrupts muscle spasms and restores full range of motion to each joint
- Erases tension from your muscles and gives you a fresh attitude

Here is a good way to stretch: Move away from your chair and stand in good posture. Stretch your right arm to the sky, stretching it until it is tight. Repeat with your left arm.

Now do your "shower exercises." These are fun exercises that you will find at the end of this chapter (page 19). They will tone and refresh your upper back and neck.

If your lower back feels tight, try this technique to loosen it up. Sit in your chair, lean over from the waist, and put your head down near your knees. Let your arms fall toward the floor. Hang there for 60 seconds. Your back muscles will relax, and you will feel yourself sinking down several more inches. Your face will probably end up in front of your knees. Sit up slowly into perfect posture. Maintaining your good posture, stand up.

During your break, move around the house using different muscles than you have been using while quilting. Unloading the dishwasher is a perfect way to use different muscles. You'll bend to reach your clean dishes and stretch to put them away.

If you feel very tired when it's time for your break, lie down in your recliner for a few minutes. The recliner will support your tired upper and lower back, as well as giving your legs, which have been working hard anchoring your pelvis, a much-needed break.

Nutrition

Eat a well-balanced diet to provide the essential nutrients your back needs to repair itself from day-to-day trauma and to build strong postural muscles.

You will find more on nutrition in Chapter 13 on page 82.

Your Quiltmaking Seats

Quiltmaking requires hours and hours of sitting, whether you use a machine or do your work by hand. A seat that fits your body precisely is essential if you want a comfortable and pain-free back.

THE CHAIR AT YOUR SEWING MACHINE The most important issues are:
- You can rest your feet flat on the floor
- Your knees make a 90° angle
- You have good lumbar support

A secretarial chair, without arm rests, is a perfect choice for machine work. These chairs can be adjusted to fit you perfectly.

See the photo on page 99.

 Buy a used secretarial chair, or find an inexpensive one at an office superstore.

RECLINERS These comfortable chairs are excellent for handwork, as they support your whole back and rest your legs as well. If your recliner lacks lumbar support, you can add it with a small, firm cushion or a rolled-up towel.

Customizing Your Sofa or Upholstered Chair to Fit Your Body

Many quiltmakers do handwork while sitting on the sofa or in an upholstered chair. These seats can be modified to fit your body precisely.

It is crucial that your feet have a flat surface to push against so they can help your legs stabilize your pelvis. If your sofa is too tall to let you rest your feet flat on the floor, you will need a firm foot support to raise your feet to a height where your thigh bones are parallel to the ground. Use a book or a firm cushion.

Finally, you will need firm lumbar support from pillows or a rolled-up towel. Place the cushion or towel above your buttocks into the curve of your back.

Selecting Quilting Projects You Love

Happy satisfied workers suffer fewer back injuries. If you make quilts that you do not like, you will be vulnerable to back injury.

Certain Medical Conditions

There are several medical or physical conditions that predispose you to back pain. If you have one or more of the following conditions, approach your quiltmaking with a strategic eye so you can pace yourself and avoid behaviors that will injure you.

HYPERMOBILITY OF JOINTS Hypermobility of the joints, also called double-jointedness, allows your joints to bend unnaturally far when your muscles contract or when you passively bend them. This bending overstretches your muscles, tendons, and ligaments. Overstretched muscles are subject to fatigue and microtrauma. If you are hypermobile, you must be very careful to customize your workspace to fit your body. Breaks every 30 minutes and cautious and gentle stretching are essential for you. Avoid overstretching.

OBESITY Obesity places a special burden on your back because your arms "wing out" to reach around your extra girth. This strains the muscles, tendons, ligaments, and joints in your back and shoulders. Also, your abdominal muscles stretch out because of the extra fat in your abdomen. This leads to back pain because strong abdominal muscles are needed to stabilize your lower back and prevent back strain.

If you are overweight, frequent breaks with stretching, use of a multivitamin, and careful attention to seating will all help to limit problems with your back.

SLENDERNESS Being underweight or naturally tiny results in small muscles. Small muscles have to do the same work that larger ones do. To protect your muscles from strain and pain, take breaks every 30 minutes. Stretch carefully.

AGE If you are over the age of 40, you have less elastic body tissues than younger quilters. Your muscles, tendons, and ligaments are more susceptible to microscopic tears from overuse. Aging muscles and ligaments also stay sore longer and aging joints ache longer. Frequent breaks, stretching, and good nutrition will help ensure you of a pain-free and comfortable back.

PREGNANCY OR THE USE OF HORMONE REPLACEMENT THERAPY Both pregnancy and the use of supplemental hormones can cause fluid retention; this stiffens your muscles, tendons, and ligaments, and leads to an increase in workload for your muscles and increased susceptibility to tears. Pace your work carefully if you are pregnant or are using hormone replacement therapy. Take breaks and take your vitamins. See Chapters 6, 7, and 8 for more on hormone-influenced times in a woman's life.

Simple Exercises for Strengthening Your Back

All muscles need exercise to stay healthy. If you do the following exercises several times a day for one month, your postural muscles will be restored to their normal size. Good posture will then become easy for you. The first exercise is done when you are still in bed. There are five more exercises to be done during your morning shower and while you are quilting.

GOOD MORNING BACK! This exercise will strengthen your lower back and create a strong and healthy platform for good posture. Lie on your back with your knees bent and your feet flat on the bed. Flatten your lower back against the bed for a slow count of ten. Release. Repeat five times. Notice the tightening of your tummy muscles and lower back muscles while you do this. Paying attention to the muscles while you exercise increases the effectiveness of all of the exercises.

After a few days, begin to lift your head off of the bed while you do the tightening. This will increase the workload of your tummy muscles and make the exercise more effective.

No matter how de-conditioned your tummy and back muscles are, they will begin to improve the first day you begin to exercise. They will get stronger every time you do this exercise.

NOTE: If you have back or neck pain, call your doctor before you start these exercises. You will probably be able to get her okay over the phone. If any of the exercises cause you pain or dizziness, stop the exercise and call your doctor.

"SHOWER EXERCISES" These exercises are just as simple as the one above. Do them for the first time each day while you stand under a hot shower. The hot water will help to stretch and condition your muscles for the day's work. For the first month, you will do these exercises once each hour while you are quilting. After that, do them once a day and whenever your back needs unkinking. You can do these exercises when you are seated at your machine. Try them right now, in the chair where you are sitting.

Yes Stand or sit in wonderful posture, with your head, shoulders, and hips in one straight line. Tuck in your chin, and be sure your shoulders are relaxed. Now gently move your chin downward until it presses against your chest. Slowly tip it back as far as it will go. Repeat three times.

No Start with your head level and your chin tucked in. Now turn as far as you can toward your right, pause, then turn as far as you can to your left. Do this twice.

Maybe-So Stand tall with your chin tucked in. Shrug your shoulders up until they are level with your ear lobes. Hold for a count of two, then let them drop. Repeat twice. Become aware of how relaxed your shoulders feel after you do this exercise.

Shoulder Rolls Stand tall and relaxed in good posture. Make a backward circle with your shoulders, returning to your starting position of perfect posture. Repeat twice.

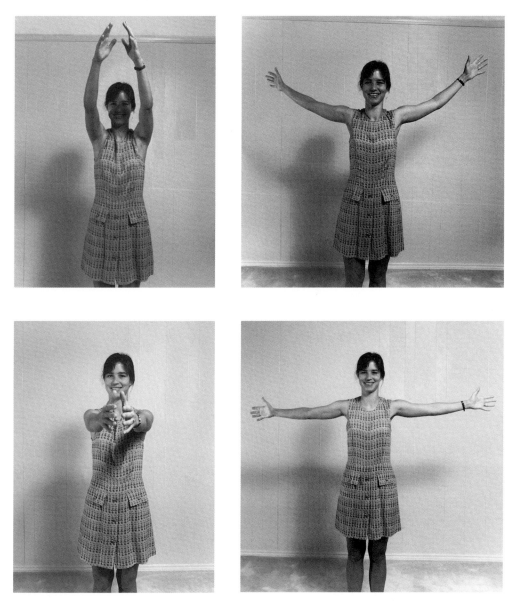

ANGELS This exercise will really help you with your posture. Beginning with good posture, lift your arms forward and upward. Your hands should be about six inches apart. Keeping your hands at this level, sweep your "wings" in an arc as far back as you can. Say "A." Return to the front and drop your hands about six inches. Repeat the movement with your hands at the new, lower level. Say "N." Continue dropping your hands six inches each time until you have spelled out ANGEL.

Further Reading I have selected two titles. I chose them because they have photographs of ordinary people doing back strengthening exercises. You will find that "back" books sometimes contradict one another. Take what seems sensible and true from any book you read, including this one, and leave the rest behind. *The Fit Back*, Time-Life Books and *The Better Back Book* by Constance Bean.

Your library will have many books on caring for your back. To find them, look under these subject words: **back, backache, abdomen-muscles, pain, exercise,** and **ergonomics.**

Avoid a Pain in the Neck

2

Comfortable, pain-free shoulders, neck, and upper back are possible for almost every quiltmaker. In this chapter we will explore:
• How to hold your head to insure pain-free shoulders, neck, and upper back
• How your head posture affects your hands and wrists
• How ill-fitting brassieres and heavy shoulder bags contribute to neck and shoulder pain

We will also look at two painful shoulder conditions that plague quilters:
• Bursitis
• Frozen shoulder

Head Posture when Quilting

Keep your head in a straight line with your shoulders and hips. Avoid craning your neck forward to see your work. Craning forward injures the nerves that operate your hands and wrists. This leads to pain, weakness, and loss of hand sensation. Also, if you crane forward for long periods, your vertebrae will gradually change shape and you will develop a "dowager's hump." Instead of craning your neck forward:
• Wear your glasses
• Secure additional lighting
• Use a magnifier

This is crucial if you spend long hours hand quilting, using your sewing machine, or using a long-arm quilting machine. Chapter 5 (page 42) discusses these solutions in detail.

Reading in Bed

Most quilters keep a stack of quilt books beside their beds for pre-sleep browsing. It's a great way to relax. If you read in bed, make sure you have enough pillows so that you can create a "wedge" of support for your head, shoulders, and back. This way you will not need to crane your neck forward. If you have a wrist injury due to repetitive movements, prop your book on a pillow instead of holding it in your hands.

Phone Posture

Many quilters chat on the phone while they machine piece or while they do handwork. Unfortunately, cradling the phone between your ear and shoulder can cause serious damage to your hand and wrist nerves. This can cause pain and loss of function. Cradling the phone between your ear and shoulder can also permanently reshape your neck vertebrae. If this happens, you may need neck surgery.

If you want to talk on the phone while you sew, invest in a headset or use a speakerphone.

The Carpal Tunnel Syndrome Connection

If you crane your neck forward to see your work, or if you cradle the phone between your head and shoulder while you stitch, your vertebrae will crush and damage the nerves that serve each hand and wrist.

One of the nerves that serves your hand travels through a tunnel in the wrist called the carpal tunnel. The repetitive movements of hand quilting can injure this nerve and cause a problem called carpal tunnel syndrome. If the nerve has already been crushed in your neck, your carpal tunnel syndrome will be unusually severe and persistent. See Chapter 3 (page 26) for more about this syndrome.

Your Bra

Seventy percent of quilters wear the wrong size bra. This can lead to neck and shoulder pain that affects quiltmaking. You owe it to yourself, to your neck, and to your shoulders to have your bra size evaluated by an expert fitter.

Shoulder Bags

A heavy shoulder bag can cause neck and shoulder misery, especially if you carry it all day at a quilt show. Shoulder bags throw off your posture. If you must carry a shoulder bag, it should weigh less than three pounds. Other solutions would be to use a waist-pack or a small purse with a strap worn across your chest.

Bursitis

Your shoulder is a wonderfully complex joint that allows you to move your arm in almost any direction. It contains several fluid filled, anti-friction sacs called bursa. Sometimes these become inflamed and painful. Bursitis can be caused by:

- Weak, unconditioned shoulder muscles
- Improper position of your arm when piecing or quilting
- Using a design wall or quilt frame for too many hours per day
- Exposure to cold

Bursitis is very painful. Treatment focuses on pain relief, decreasing inflammation, and on correcting the underlying cause of the disorder. The following can help you to make these corrections:

- Build up your shoulder muscles by holding small soup cans in your hands when you do the "Angel" exercise on page 21. This is especially important if you use a design wall frequently or if you quilt using a frame.
- Try piecing or quilting while resting your forearms on a surface that is at elbow height when you are seated. Your kitchen table may work for this.
- Avoid using your design wall or quilt frame for more than two hours a day. If you must work longer, take a break every 30 minutes.
- Keep your arms and shoulders warm when you use your design wall or quilt frame.

Frozen Shoulder

Sometimes the hormonal fluctuations of the perimenopause lead to changes in the fibrous tissues in the shoulder. This results in severe pain when you move your arm. It is natural to avoid these painful movements. Unfortunately, if you stop using your arm, your shoulder will "freeze up" and lose its mobility.

The first part of the solution to the problem of "frozen shoulder" is to restore the full range of movement to your shoulder. A physical therapist or a licensed massage therapist can do this for you. After movement in your shoulder is restored it is important to move your arm through its full range of movements every day, even when it hurts. One good way to do this is to put on and remove a snug-fitting tee shirt twice every morning and twice every evening.

Further Reading: Your library will have more on the topics in this chapter. Start with subject words: **shoulder pain, neck pain, backache, pain,** and **ergonomics**.

3 Carpal Tunnel Syndrome & Other Repetitive Strain Injuries

One in ten quilters will develop carpal tunnel syndrome. This chapter describes the disorder and its causes and addresses some of the lifestyle changes that can prevent you from developing the disorder. If you already have carpal tunnel syndrome, these lifestyle changes can bring about an immediate improvement in the condition. This chapter also discusses rotary cutters and a type of repetitive strain injury (RSI) related to their use.

Symptoms of Carpal Tunnel Syndrome

Carpal tunnel syndrome (CTS) announces itself with burning pain on the palm side of your thumb, index finger, and middle finger. You might also experience a diffuse aching of your wrist and forearm. The burning-tingling pain is often worse at night.

Course and Prognosis

If untreated, the condition often progresses with increasing pain, and shrinkage and weakness of your hand muscles. Severe cases that go untreated can result in permanent nerve damage, with irreversible loss of sensation and strength of the hand.

THE CARPAL TUNNEL The carpal tunnel is in your wrist, just under the spot where you put your fingers to take your pulse. Nine tendons and the median nerve travel through the tunnel. A strong ligament roofs it.

Why CTS Develops

Movements that flex your wrist, such as hand quilting, slide the nerve and tendons back and forth in the carpal tunnel and exhaust your body's natural lubricants. This injures the nerve, tendons, and ligaments in your carpal tunnel. The pain, weakness, and muscle wasting of carpal tunnel syndrome occur because of injury to the nerve.

Risk Factors

The wrist movements required by quilting and by some jobs and hobbies put you at risk for a repetitive strain injury such as carpal tunnel syndrome. If you do any of the following for more than 2 hours per day, you are at risk for CTS:

- Quilt or do other needlework
- Use a computer
- Play a musical instrument
- Cut hair

There are four other important risk factors:

- Being premenstrual, i.e., in the time just before your period
- Being pregnant
- Being a woman over 40
- Having a square wrist rather than a flat, oval one

Prevention

If you are at risk, you must pay special attention to these lifestyle and technique issues:

- Excellent posture
- Good hand quilting technique
- Use of a workstation adjusted to fit your body
- Having a balanced workload with adequate rest periods

I will show you easy and fun ways you can do all of the above.

EXCELLENT POSTURE Sit upright with your head, shoulders, and hips in one straight line. Maintain this posture in a relaxed way. Good head and shoulder posture will protect your median nerve from the "double crush syndrome" where the median nerve is crushed once in the neck and again in the carpal tunnel.

Never cradle the phone between your ear and shoulder, as this is guaranteed to crush your hand nerves as they travel in your neck. Never crane forward to see your work. Sit up straight and be sure you have enough light to see clearly. Wear your glasses. If you maintain good neck posture, you will never have to worry about double crush injury. See Chapter 2 for more on head posture (page 23). For more on task lighting, see page 43.

Your feet should be flat on the floor. Your forearms should make a right angle to your body and your wrists should be straight. Your quilting frame, quilting hoop, and sewing machine must allow for this or you will put stress on your carpal tunnel.

The rocking technique requires you to bend your wrist.

Thumb quilting allows your wrist to remain straight.

If you turned to this chapter first, please read Chapters 1 and 2 for a thorough discussion of posture and to learn fun and easy exercises that you can do as you work to assure healthy, postural muscles and problem-free wrists.

HAND QUILTING TECHNIQUE Most quilters use the rocking technique when hand quilting. In the rocking technique, you use a thimble on your middle finger and bend your wrist to quilt toward yourself.

Using the rocking technique puts you at great risk for developing carpal tunnel syndrome. If you learn to quilt with your thumb, you will be able to keep your wrist straight while you quilt.

Ease into thumb quilting by doing it half of the time. Wear a regular thimble on your middle finger and a leather thimble on your thumb. My favorites are Clover's Coin Thimble® and the Nimble Thimble®.

Use your regular thimble to quilt toward yourself and your thumb thimble to quilt away from yourself. This will rest your wrist half of the time.

You will notice that you can quilt twice as fast with your thumb. Within a month, you will probably prefer your thumb thimble. Once you are quilting exclusively with a thumb thimble, your wrist will be straight all of the time that you quilt.

The Quilter's Thimble®, a flat thimble that you hold in your hand, is another tool that allows you to keep your wrist straight when you quilt.

An Ergonomic Workstation

Ergonomics is a new science that adjusts the workstation to fit the worker. Use the following instructions to find the perfect height for your sewing machine. This is crucial for the health of your hands, wrists, shoulders, and neck.

Find the correct height for your sewing chair by using the guidelines in Chapter 1 on page 16. Once you have adjusted your chair to its proper height, you will be able to calculate the correct height for your sewing machine.

To find the correct height for your machine:
- Sit in your sewing chair.
- Use a yardstick to measure the   of your bent elbow to the floor. This is the corre   ɡs of your sewing machine. (Measurement #1.)
- Measure the thickness of the ba   urement #2.)
- Subtract the second measureme   lt is the correct height for your sewing machine t

The photo on page 99 shows a sew   height for the quilter using it. Most tables are too h   ..d as a temporary table for your machine and try ou   ...ɡht you calculated. When you are satisfied with the height, buy an oversized, adjustable TV table to hold your machine or cut down an old table to the correct height.

Measurement #1, above, is the correct height for your freestanding hoop or your quilting frame. If you are overweight, the thickness of your legs may force your table to be too high for optimum wrist health. Compromise by lowering your work surface as much as possible.

ERGONOMIC PRODUCTS There are not yet any federal standards for use of the label "ergonomic." Some "ergonomic" products are good for one part of the body, but can be harmful to another part of the body. An example is a popular tilting platform for your sewing machine. This product is wonderful for quilters with cervical neck disease. However, this device forces you to bend your wrists. This can worsen carpal tunnel syndrome.

You will *not* need "ergonomic" doodads for sewing if you:
- Adjust your sewing chair and sewing machine to the proper heights for you.
- Stabilize your hips by putting your feet flat on the floor and by maintaining good head posture.
- Provide good lighting and wear your glasses.

A BALANCED WORKLOAD WITH ADEQUATE REST PERIODS Allow yourself plenty of time to complete each quilting task. Do not engage in marathon rotary cutting, marathon machine sewing, or marathon hand quilting.

Marathons overstress your body's healing mechanisms and can lead to serious injury.

Take 10-minute breaks every hour. If you have carpal tunnel syndrome or another repetitive strain injury, take a 10-minute break every 30 minutes.

Your breaks should include careful stretching to restore your muscles to their proper length and to erase any tension buildup from your quiltmaking session. See page 15 for more on breaks and stretching.

INSTANT CARPAL TUNNEL SYNDROME A friend developed the classic symptoms of carpal tunnel syndrome in just one week. She had spent about four hours a day machine quilting her entry for a show. She placed her machine on her dining room table to help support the quilt while she worked. Unfortunately, her table was four inches higher than the correct height for her body. To make matters worse, the light was poor in her dining room so she sat hunched over, with her face near the needle—instant double crush injury.

If You Think You May Already Have Carpal Tunnel Syndrome

If you believe you have carpal tunnel syndrome, see your doctor for a thorough examination.

DIAGNOSIS Your doctor will evaluate the seriousness of your condition and rule out any medical causes of the disorder, such as diabetes, rheumatoid arthritis, or hypothyroidism.

In addition to taking a medical history, your doctor may perform a physical exam including tapping on your wrist and holding your wrist in a bent position for several moments. She may also order blood tests and nerve conduction tests. Taken together, these will tell her how far the syndrome has progressed. The treatment she prescribes will depend on the severity of your condition.

TREATMENTS In mild, early cases, your doctor will prescribe a combination of:
- Rest
- Painkillers
- Ice

These will be discussed in detail later in this chapter. She will also prescribe lifestyle changes including good posture, better technique, and equipment that fits you.

Moderate nerve damage will be treated with all of the above, plus splinting or casting. Moderate CTS is sometimes treated with steroid injection.

Severe cases, when the nerve damage is close to being permanent, may require immediate surgery to decompress the nerve. In the last few years, there have been some significant advances in surgery for carpal tunnel syndrome. These techniques use very small incisions and have rapid healing times.

After surgery, do not fail to make the lifestyle changes your doctor recommends. Otherwise you may find yourself back in the operating room in 18 months.

Other medical treatments for carpal tunnel syndrome can include:

- Spinal manipulation to restore proper neck alignment. This treatment might be important if you have a "double crush injury."
- Massage to relax you and to promote healing of the injured soft tissues
- Ultrasound to increase blood flow and to decrease pain and inflammation
- An occupational therapy consultation to analyze your activities, to do postural training, to make ergonomic adjustments to your work area, and to create splints to protect your joints as you work

Your doctor will be your "case manager" and will refer you to any other practitioners you need.

REST A broken bone will usually heal in about four weeks with rest and immobilization. Unfortunately, your soft tissues do not heal as quickly. Carpal tunnel syndrome or other repetitive strain injuries may take four months, or longer, to heal.

- The good news takes two forms:
  1. You get to keep using your hands while you heal.
  2. Lifestyle changes will almost always bring about an improvement in your symptoms.
- The bad news is, if you keep making the same mistakes about posture, technique, equipment, and rest, your wrists will continue to get worse.
- The amount and degree of rest your doctor prescribes will depend on the severity of your injury. Listen carefully to her advice. The future of your hands depends on following her advice.

PAINKILLERS The pain of carpal tunnel syndrome can be disabling. It is often much worse at night, for reasons we shall see in the following paragraphs. Some doctors recommend the use of a simple analgesic such as Tylenol, which reduces pain without affecting the injured tissues.

Other doctors prescribe non-steroidal anti-inflammatory drugs, such as Motrin or Advil. These drugs act directly in the injured tissues. Use of non-steroidal anti-inflammatory drugs (NSAIDs) in repetitive strain injury is controversial. Many orthopedic surgeons believe these drugs actually increase microscopic scarring in the injured structures.

I stand with the doctors who believe NSAIDs are harmful in repetitive strain injuries. I believe the solution to the problem lies in respectful use of the body. I recommend Tylenol for acute pain, such as you might incur after "bingeing" on quiltmaking at a retreat. Discuss this with your own doctor before you decide whether to use NSAIDs for symptoms of carpal tunnel syndrome.

ICING Current medical wisdom uses ice for new or chronic injury. Ice packs applied to the aching areas of the hands and wrist for 10 to 15 minutes can help control pain and swelling. Use ice wrapped in a towel or a can of chilled soda for this purpose.

SPLINTS Splints can be very helpful because they give your wrist a rest from bending. Many quilters with carpal tunnel syndrome use a splint at night. Splints can be wonderful tools for healing because almost everyone flexes her wrists during sleep. Splints eliminate eight hours of bending each day and provide eight extra hours of healing. An ideal splint is very stiff. It allows you about 10% of your normal wrist movement and, of course, allows for good blood flow. You can buy one at a large pharmacy or at a medical supply store. No prescription is needed. Splints cost less than $15.

- Use a Rollerblade wrist guard for a splint
- Create a soft splint with an Ace® wrap or Quilter's Wrap®

CRAFT GLOVES Using craft gloves is controversial. Many doctors believe using craft gloves when bending your wrist is harmful because the gloves can weaken your muscles.

The solutions to CTS and other repetitive strain injuries are excellent posture, good technique, proper equipment, and a balanced workload.

VITAMINS Some scientists believe carpal tunnel syndrome is related to a deficiency of Vitamin B6. Many quilters have healed their CTS by using vitamin supplements. If you have carpal tunnel syndrome and if your doctor okays it, take the following supplements daily for twelve weeks and see if it helps:
- Vitamin B6-50 mg. (or use Vitamin B-complex, 50 mg.)
- Vitamin C-100 mg.
- Vitamin E-800 I.U.
- A multivitamin with minerals

THE LAST WORD ON CARPAL TUNNEL SYNDROME If you do not change your quilting lifestyle, the damage to your wrist will continue.

Rotary Cutting and "Pizza Cutters' Palsy"

This chapter would not be complete without a discussion about rotary cutters and the damage they can do to the nerves of your hand. This has been studied in pizza makers.

Pizza makers use rotary cutters with narrow handles that press into the soft tissues of their palms. Some pizza makers have developed paralysis of their thumbs and index fingers as a result of trauma to a nerve in their palms. The damage is reversed when they switch to a padded rotary cutter, which spreads the force of cutting over a wider area.

This has important implications for quiltmakers. If you use a rotary cutter for fabric and you have weakness in your thumb and index finger, see your doctor right away.

The newer rotary cutters have fat, padded handles, and should not cause this problem. If you have an older, thin-handled rotary cutter, try one of these solutions:

- Wrap the handle thickly in electrical tape or padded handlebar tape.
- Protect the nerve in your palm by using a padded, fingerless bicycling glove when you cut.

HOW LONG CAN YOU ROTARY CUT SAFELY? Rotary cutting is hard on your hand, wrist, forearm, shoulder, and back.

- Do not cut more than two hours per day.
- Take 10-minute breaks every hour. Take breaks more often if your arm or back get tired.
- If you are ambidextrous, alternate cutting hands every 15 minutes when you are cutting.

CARE AND USE OF YOUR ROTARY CUTTER There are some simple things you can do to limit the strain which rotary cutting puts on your hand, arm, and shoulder.

- Use your large-sized blade for cutting fabric strips.
- Replace your blade after every large cutting project. Save used blades for resharpening.
- Loosen the blade a little so it rolls more easily.
- Oil the area under the screw so the blade turns with less friction.
- Clear your work surface of pins. A nicked blade will require you to make many more arm movements.

YOUR ROTARY CUTTING MAT Several quiltmakers with repetitive strain injury have written to say that the white Salem® mats are easier on their injured forearms. If you have RSI and do a lot of rotary cutting, you might want to borrow different mats from your quilting friends and test them to find the one that is best for you.

Quiltmaking When You Have Work-related RSI

When your work has left you with serious RSI and you want to spend time quilting, you will have some very tough decisions to make. Quiltmaking requires you to make repetitive movements of your injured muscles and tendons. You will have to evaluate a host of factors, including:

- Your need to use your hands to make a living
- Which lifestyle changes you are willing to make
- How much permanent injury you are willing to accept as the result of overusing your hands

Only you can decide what to do. Chapter 10: Personal Injury or Illness—Embracing Change, on page 67, may be helpful to you as you consider your options.

Further Reading If you have carpal tunnel syndrome, or another repetitive strain injury, do yourself the favor of reading more about it.

I highly recommend the following title: *Repetitive Strain Injury: A Computer User's Guide* by Emil Pascarelli, M.D., and Deborah Quilter.

Your library will have more books on the topics in this chapter. To find them look under these subject words: **carpal tunnel syndrome, repetitive strain injury, RSI, overuse injuries, stress management, pain,** and **ergonomics.**

Sore Fingers

4

Do your fingers become sore when you quilt or piece? If so, this chapter shows you why they get sore and shares techniques and tools to help you to minimize the soreness.

Two Causes of Finger Soreness

The soreness in your fingertips has two main causes:
- Needle pricks
- "Bruising"

Needle Pricks

When you hand quilt, the needle pierces your finger every time you take a stitch. Your needle also slices your finger as it rocks toward its upward swing.

Your needle carries skin bacteria and fibers from your fabric into your fingertip. Your blood vessels dilate in response and carry:
- Construction materials needed to repair your finger
- White cells that fight infection and remove debris from the injury

The pain from needle-pricks comes from three sources:
- Trauma from the needle
- White cell by-products
- Dilation of blood vessels

"Bruising"

When you hold a needle for several hours a day, the pressure and movement will cause fluid to seep out of your blood vessels into your finger pads. Your finger pads contain lymph vessels to carry away this fluid. However, if you haven't been stitching recently, it will take several days for them to begin to work efficiently. Until then, your fingers will feel bruised from the accumulation of fluid.

✓ **SOLUTIONS** There are quite a few things you can do to minimize both types of finger soreness.

Your Quilting Callus

Your body provides you with an excellent barrier to the needle: your quilting callus. The surface of your skin is made up of flat, dead skin cells. This layer will become thicker and form a callus if you quilt every day. Your callus will provide a way for your healthy, vital skin to sense the needle without the needle piercing your living tissue. Your callus also provides a pain-free zone through which your needle can "rock."

CALLUS CARE HINTS
- Your quilting callus requires care so it can remain in good condition. Provide moisture and oil to keep it soft and supple. Every time you wet your hands, seal in the moisture by applying lotion or "Quilting Cream." You will find a recipe for Quilting Cream on page 37.
- Your callus will be very soft for 30 minutes after your hands have been wet. Take great care if you quilt during this time or you may suffer deep needle pricks.
- Avoid direct contact with ammonia-containing products or chlorine-based scouring powders when you have a good quilting callus. These products strip moisture and oils from your callus. Use gloves or plastic bags on your hands when you must use these products.
- Smooth your quilting callus with a drop of lemon juice. The acid in the juice will restructure and smooth it. Alternately, buff your callus lightly with a pumice stone.
- Quilting carries surface dirt into your finger. Have a tetanus booster every 10 years.

Pain Relief for Sore Fingers

- Doing dishes in comfortably warm water will help to soothe and heal your sore fingers. The warm water will stimulate circulation in your fingers and facilitate the arrival of white cells and repair materials.
- Stop quilting when the pain becomes severe. Pain is your body's way of telling you to rest your fingers.
- As you move through your day, massage your sore fingertips with your thumb. Massage a little "First Days" Quilting Cream into your fingertips. The recipe is given on the following page.
- Quilters have appropriated several veterinary products to soothe their sore fingers. Unfortunately, no government agency has approved them for human use. They include Bag Balm®, Udder Cream®, and Hoof Quencher®.
- Several quiltmakers wrote to say that they rub their "under the quilt" fingers with turpentine at the end of the quilting day to decrease soreness.

Quilting Cream

Many quiltmakers have written to tell me how much they love my "Quilting Cream." Mix some and keep it above your kitchen sink and in your bathroom. When you are quilting, use it every time you wet your hands.

Before you use the Quilting Cream, do patch tests to see if you are allergic to any of the three ingredients. Write the names of the ingredients on separate Band-Aids®. Place a dab of each ingredient on its Band-Aid. Apply the Band-Aids to your forearm at bedtime. In the morning, remove them and check for redness. If your skin is reddened under any of the Band-Aids, avoid using that ingredient. Also note that if excess cream gets onto your quilt, it can stain. Wipe your fingers carefully before sitting down to quilt after your break.

The following recipes are approximate. Mix together a little of each ingredient.

"FIRST DAYS" QUILTING CREAM You can use this recipe for the first few days you quilt, before your callus forms. The antibiotic will help to kill the bacteria your needle will carry into your finger. Squeeze out about 1" of each of the following and mix them together with your finger:

- Bacitracin® Ointment—Bacitracin can be found in large drug stores. Do not use Polysporin® or Neosporin®, as these cause frequent allergic reactions.
- Vitamin A and D Ointment®—You probably used this on your baby's bottom. It is loaded with the vitamins your skin needs. If you do not care for the odor, you can substitute A and D Cream®.
- Cuticle Cream—Large drug stores carry this. It will moisturize your callus and keep it supple.

MAINTENANCE QUILTING CREAM Once your callus forms, you can use equal parts of Vitamin A and D ointment and cuticle cream or cuticle cream alone.

Rub "Quilting Cream" into your sore fingers. I keep mine in my grandmother's cut glass salt cellars.

Bruised Fingers

This soreness is like the saddle soreness you feel when you ride your bike for the first time each spring. If you want to avoid the pain, try the following tip:

ANTICIPATORY FINGER MASSAGE Eliminate much of the soreness of bruising by getting your fingers to open up their blood and lymph vessels *before you start to piece or quilt.*

Gently massage your right index and middle fingers by rubbing them with your right thumb. Do this for about 30 seconds every hour. This will prepare both your fingers and thumb for holding the needle.

Preventing Needle Prick Injuries

Preventing needle pricks is your first line of defense against finger soreness. Barriers can be natural such as your callus or they can be mechanical. Good mechanical barriers include:

- Thimble-It® and Thimble Pad® are self-adhesive needle barriers. Thimble-Its are supple plastic ovals and Thimble Pads are round leather dots. These work like natural calluses, but peel off after every quilting session. They are so comfortable that you might forget you are wearing one.
- The UnderThimble® is a metal surface that attaches to your fingertip by an adhesive dot. These prevent most needle pricks and are a good choice for diabetics and chemotherapy patients. They are also good for older quilters and others whose fingers heal slowly.
- Quilter's Wrap® and Wrap-a-Finger® are stretchy, self-sticking wraps. They form an "Ace wrap" for the fingertips.
- Tape. Use masking tape, surgeon's tape, or a dot of tape cut from a Band-Aid.
- Nail Polish. Paint a coat of clear nail polish onto the spot where your needle hits. Moisturize your fingertip after you remove the polish.

Your Piecing Needles

There are several things you can do to make the first days of piecing easier on your fingers.

- Use milliner's needles for hand piecing. Their tiny shafts will slip through your fabric easily. If you have trouble threading milliner's needles, try John James® #9 long darners.
- Use your "old," well-broken-in needles as you begin to piece. They will already be curved to fit your fingers.

Your Quilting Needles

Try these tricks before you begin quilting your next project:

- Use the smallest quilting needles possible. They will slip through the fabric more easily. The higher the number of the needle, the smaller its shaft.
- Experiment with platinum-coated needles. These move through your quilt with less friction, which means less wear and tear on your fingers.
- Use curved, well-broken-in needles the first few days of quilting.
- Select the thinnest batt that works for your project.
- For the first few days, avoid loading up your needle with stitches. Take two or three stitches and pull the needle through. You can take more stitches when your fingers are toned up.

More on Finger Pain

There are two other sources of finger pain in the quiltmaking process: your basting pins and finger burns from hot fabric.

YOUR BASTING PINS   If you experience pain when opening or closing your 1" basting pins, try these tips:

- Use a notched spoon-tool or a Kwik Klip® to fasten and unfasten your safety pins.
- If you have a large ring size, or if your fingers are swollen due to pregnancy or illness, using larger pins will reduce the pain. Buy $1^1/_2$" pins or 2" pins.
- If you are an older quilter, you will appreciate the larger pins because the tips of your fingers have less padding than they had when you were younger. Larger size pins cause much less pain.
- Try a basting gun, which shoots plastic "tacks" to hold the layers of your quilt together. Test on your fabric first, as it can leave holes.
- If you have hand or wrist problems, ask your small group to help you baste your quilt. Save your hands for tasks you love, such as hand quilting.

IRONING TIPS If you make miniature quilts, or if you make bias strips for appliqué, try these ideas to protect your fingers from burns resulting from touching hot fabric.

- Wear an all-leather thimble on your left index finger to protect it from heat and steam.
- Buy a pair of inexpensive close-fitting leather gloves at a thrift store or an antique mall. Cut off the ring and baby fingers of the left glove. Wear the left glove when you must handle very hot fabric.
- Wear a Cool Fingers® knitted finger protector or make a finger protector by removing one finger from an old pair of gardening gloves. Knitted finger protectors will not safeguard you from steam burns.

Tips for Quilters with Diabetes, Raynaud's Disorder, Peripheral Vascular Disease, or Quilters having Chemotherapy

If you have one of these conditions, your fingers will heal slowly. You may also be more prone to infection. Try these hints to minimize these risks:

- Use an antibacterial liquid dishwashing detergent. This will minimize the number of bacteria carried into your finger by the needle.
- Maximize blood flow to your fingers by massaging your fingertips every time you take a break.
- Set a lazy pace for the completion of the quilting. Give your fingers all the time they need to heal.

Tips for Quiltmakers with Scleroderma or Other Conditions that Stiffen the Fingers

Stiff fingers can interfere with quilting. Try these ideas if you suffer from finger stiffness.

- If finger stiffness prevents you from using the rocking stitch, try the stab stitch. Stab your needle straight down through the quilt layers, passing it all the way through your quilt. Now pass it up through the quilt. With a little practice, you will be able to make tiny, beautiful stitches.
- Try Utility Quilting. Make running stitches with a large-eye needle and perle cotton. Use size 5 betweens or sharps and DMC® Number 8 perle cotton. For small projects, don't use a hoop; just quilt the piece in your hands.

Tips for Quilters with Arthritis

Arthritis can cause morning stiffness as well as joint deformity. Here are a few suggestions to help you keep quilting:

- Fill a bowl or sink with comfortably warm water. Limber up your joints by wringing out a washcloth or sponge. Repeat as needed throughout the day.
- Try thumb quilting, as described in Chapter 3, page 28.
- If joint deformity keeps you from using your fingers the way you used to, ask your doctor to refer you to an occupational therapist. She can create splints that will stabilize the joints of your fingers. It is likely that your insurance will cover these, especially if you also use the splints for "activities of daily living," such as food preparation.
- Try wrapping your sore joints with Quilter's Wrap or Wrap-a-Finger. These "soft splints" may help you to use your fingers the way you did in the past.
- Wrap your sore knuckles with a one-inch strip of Wonder Tape®.
- Try the Quilter's Thimble, a thimble you hold in your hand.

- Take a 5-minute break every 10 minutes. This will allow your joints to replenish their lubricating fluid. Use your break to wring out a sponge in warm water, as previously suggested.
- As long as you are taking frequent breaks, feel free to take the painkillers your doctor has recommended. Never substitute painkillers for breaks.

Blood on Your Quilt

Occasionally your needle will pierce you deeply and you will get blood on the back of your quilt. See Chapter 10 for three ways to remove blood from a quilt (page 71).

Sharing Needles

Sometimes at quilting bees, quiltmakers leave their needles behind when they get up to snack. Another quilter may pick up your needle and use it. If you have a blood-borne infectious disease such as hepatitis or HIV, you must not leave your quilt needles where someone else might use them. Take your needle with you when you leave the frame. You needn't reveal you are ill; simply say you use a special needle and want to keep it with you.

For More Information: References on the skin of the fingers are few and far between. Please consult your personal physician if you need more information.

5 The Eyes Have It: The Quilter's Eyes Over the Lifecycle

The Youthful Eye

Do you remember the last time that you touched the magical softness of a newborn baby's cheek? That softness is a sign that most of the fibers in the baby's body are made of a stretchy fiber called elastin. As we age, we replace soft elastin with a tougher fiber called collagen. Collagen allows our bodies to stand up to adult life tasks. It also makes all of our tissues stiffer, including the lens of the eye.

The youthful eye has a supple, flexible lens and a full complement of light receptors in the retina. It can:

- Switch from near to far vision in an instant
- Distinguish subtle contrasts
- Perform monotonous visual tasks like needlework without tiring

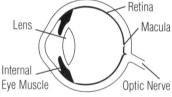

The Eye after 30

The aging eye has a stiffer, less flexible lens that has begun to yellow. If you are over the age of 30 you may begin to experience the achy tiredness of eyestrain when sewing for long periods. Although your vision might still be 20/20 on a black and white eye chart, you may begin to have problems distinguishing subtle contrasts. The sections on Sunglasses (page 47) and Nutrition (page 47) offer tips to help you to slow down these aging processes.

Eyestrain

Eyestrain is an overuse injury of the tiny muscles attached to your eyes' lenses. It leads to overuse injury of the large muscles that move your eyes inward. Symptoms include:

- Pain or tiredness of the eyes, eyelids, and forehead
- Dry, irritable eyes
- Or irritable, watery eyes
- Sensitivity to light
- Headache
- Temporary inability to focus on distant objects

Preventing eyestrain is simple:
- Have enough light.
- Think happy thoughts. If your thoughts upset you, your eyes will dilate and force your tiny inner eye muscles to work harder.
- Wear your glasses.
- Blink every 30 seconds. This lubricates and moistens your eyes and gives you a tiny visual vacation. Take 5 minutes right now to learn to blink every 30 seconds. Watch a timepiece with a sweep-second hand. Spend 5 minutes blinking every 30 seconds.
- Take a visual break every 5 minutes. For 30 seconds, look outside or look at a picture on the wall. If you are watching TV while you stitch, you do this every time you look at the screen.
- Drink a glass of water every hour. This helps flush out the buildup of lactic acid in your eye muscles and helps prevent eye muscle soreness. The extra water also helps keep your eyes lubricated and comfortable.

The Eye after 40

By the time you turn forty, no matter how far away you hold your needlework, it is hard to bring it into focus. Reading glasses or bifocals can really help. See the section on your eye exam on page 46 for tips to help you obtain a perfect prescription.

Lighting for Your Forties

If you are 40, you need 20% more light than you needed at age 30. Increase the wattage of the table lamp nearest to your handwork chair and in the ceiling fixture in your sewing room. Adding this little bit of light reduces eyestrain, makes needle eyes seem larger, and allows you to clip threads comfortably.

The Eye after 50

At 50, you sit down at your machine and your feed dogs look blurry. Looking at bolts of fabric on the shelves of your quilt shop causes an uncomfortable pulling sensation inside of your eyes. Trifocals can restore your comfort. Needles can be very hard to thread. Needle threaders can be helpful. The thing the aging eye needs the most is bright illumination.

Lighting for Your Fifties

If you are 50, you will require 50% more light. The lighting changes you make now will continue to help you into your nineties.

The extra light helps in many ways:

- Extra light effectively increases contrast. With enough artificial light, you should even be able to see well enough to clip black threads from black fabric.
- Extra light closes down the pupil in your eye. This gives your eyes' lenses a greater depth of focus and lets your tiny eye muscles rest.
- If you have lost a significant number of light receptors, more light gives the remaining light receptors a better chance to provide you with a sharp visual image.

The lighting you provide must have three qualities. It should be bright, glare-free, and shadow-free.

LIGHTING FOR YOUR HANDWORK CHAIR The chair where you do your handwork needs the best light because of the fineness of the stitching you do there—piecing, appliqué, and binding. Twin floor lamps beside your sewing chair will provide shadow-free light. Another good choice is a single torchlight placed behind or to one side of your chair. Torchlights come in both modern and classical styles. The light they produce reflects off your ceiling and provides shadowless, glare-free light.

LIGHTING FOR YOUR SEWING ROOM Your sewing room requires extra light. Buy two torchlights for your sewing room. The torchlights plus your existing ceiling fixture will create all the light you need. Or instead of torchlights, replace your ceiling fixture with a four-bulb fluorescent fixture. Choose fluorescent bulbs that approximate sunlight. The daylight bulbs will optimize your color sense and increase your sense of well-being. Ask your lighting store clerk for fluorescent tubes with 5000 degree Kelvin light. Sylvania's current designation for its daylight bulb is F40 Design 50. GE's bulbs are currently named F40C50. Both currently retail for about $7.00 per four-foot tube.

LIGHTING FOR YOUR SEWING MACHINE You may need supplemental light at your machine in your fifties. Find freestanding and clip-on sewing lamps in the catalogs mentioned in Sources on page 111.

LIGHTING WHEN SEWING IN OTHER LOCATIONS If you stitch in places where you have no control over the light intensity, buy an under the chin spotlight made for needleworkers.

The Eye after 60

Although your eyeglass prescription won't change much in this decade, contrast and visual sharpness become bigger problems.

As lens yellowing becomes more pronounced, it may be difficult for you to judge colors. Pastels and cool colors like blue and green will now take on a grayish cast. If you use these colors in your quilts, have a friend review your color choices before you buy fabric for a big project. Select someone whose color sense you trust. If you use warm colors in your quilts, you are in luck; the yellowing of your lenses will not interfere with your color choices.

- As your lenses continue to stiffen, you may have to hold your handwork exactly 16" from your eyes (the focal length of your bifocal prescription).
- Macular degeneration may be problematic in this decade. You may require a magnifier and/or a needle threader now.
- Your eyes will tire more easily. Eyestrain forces you to use more light, wear your glasses, and take frequent breaks.
- The whites of your eyes become thinner, exposing the blood vessels. The redness is not a sign of eyestrain or overuse, unless it worsens when you sew.

Lighting and Magnifiers for the Sixties (and Beyond)

At age 60, you will require 70% more light than you did at age 30. The lighting changes described above will be a good beginning. You may also need magnifying lenses in order to do handwork.

Magnifiers come in a wide variety of styles. One is sure to be perfect for you.

- Magnifiers mounted in headbands are a time-honored solution to the eye changes of the aging process. They do not work with every hairstyle.
- Around-the-neck magnifiers come with and without lights. Lighted ones come with adapters to convert between battery and AC current.
- Stand-mounted magnifiers are another time-tested solution. These come with and without lights.
- Magnifiers made to improve your view of the feed dogs on your machine are a wonderful help. These come in freestanding and clip-on models.

See the Sources on page 111.

The Eye in the Seventies (and Beyond)

Although your eyeglass prescription may not change, you will have less flexibility about where to hold your needlework. You may only be able to focus your eyes at 16" with your bifocals and 30" with your trifocals. If you like to hold your handwork at another distance, your optician can make lenses that focus at the distance you desire. Or you can use a magnifier.

Your fine vision will continue to decline. It is never too late to start the eye care hints under Eyestrain (page 42) and Nutrition (page 47).

Choosing quilt patches that have lots of contrast can really help a low-vision quiltmaker continue to work. Use red and white; deep blue and muslin, etc. Also, consider using dark colored quilting thread, which will stand out against a light colored background fabric.

Utility quilting, described in Chapter 4 (page 40), can be a wonderful compromise for low-vision quilters. One ninety-year-old was able to resume quilting after she used high contrast fabrics in her quilt, switched to utility quilting, and selected colored perle cotton for her "quilting thread."

Help for Imperfect Eyes

There are three ways to improve your useful vision:
- Corrective lenses
- Sufficient lighting and magnifiers
- Good nutrition and multivitamin supplements

Corrective Lenses

Maybe you are one of those lucky quilters who doesn't need corrective lenses. If so, skip to the sections on Sunglasses and Nutrition on the following page to learn how to keep your eyes' lenses crystal clear and the light receptors in your retinas healthy.

Your Eye Exam

There are a few things you can do to make sure your eye exam results in the best prescription possible:
- Write down any visual problems you are having, that way you won't forget to discuss them with your doctor. Write down the distance from your eye to where you hold your piecing; from your eye to your quilting hoop; and from your eye to the feed dogs on your machine. Put the list in your purse the night before your eye appointment.
- Speak frankly to your doctor about your vision problems and special needs, referring to your list and to the measurements you made at home. Make sure she understands the distances at which you need to have sharp focus when you are making quilts.
- Give thoughtful attention to the choices your doctor offers during your eye exam.
- When you go to fill your prescription for corrective lenses, take your problem list and distance measurements. Discuss your vision needs with your optician as well. He will use your doctor's prescription to create glasses that fit your needs perfectly.

Sunglasses

Ultraviolet light is the main culprit in causing your eyes' lenses to yellow. It is also the main culprit in damaging the light receptors in your retinas. You can dramatically decrease both the yellowing of your lenses and the loss of light receptors by wearing sunglasses whenever you are outside between 10 a.m. and 2 p.m. Snow and water are UV reflectors, so be sure to wear your sunglasses on bright days in snow or on the water.

 Whenever I get new prescription glasses, I have the optician convert my old glasses to sunglasses by tinting the old lenses. It only costs a few dollars.

I recommend sunglasses that screen out 99% of the UV-A and UV-B. These sunglasses will have one of the following labels:

- Blocks 99% of ultraviolet rays
- Meets ANSI UV requirements
- UV absorption up to 40nm
- Special Purpose

 Sunglasses meeting these requirements can cost as little as $10. Any large drugstore carries them.

Nutrition and Eye Health

Twenty percent of quilters have at least one eye symptom due to vitamin deficiency. These can include dry eyes, blurred vision, eye pain, and macular degeneration. Many eye symptoms will improve if you will take a multivitamin with minerals each day.

Some Special Eye Conditions Affecting Quiltmaking

There are three serious eye conditions that can adversely influence your quiltmaking: cataracts, glaucoma, and diabetic retinopathy. Regular visits to your ophthalmologist, the use of sunglasses, and good nutrition can all help you to avoid these vision robbers.

Cataracts

A cataract is a clouding of the lens of the eye. Cataracts can form as a result of the aging process, as a result of eye trauma, or as a complication of diabetes.

Symptoms include fogged vision, headaches, and seeing a halo around objects. Under ordinary conditions, cataracts will not be treated until they interfere with daily life or work. Treatment usually consists of removing the cloudy lens and implanting a clear plastic one. Ninety percent of patients who have cataract surgery recover useful vision.

Glaucoma

Glaucoma is a serious eye disease that can cause blindness if left untreated. Two percent of quilters over age 35 have this disorder. When diagnosed early and treated, vision can almost always be saved. Glaucoma causes an increase in fluid pressure inside the eyeball. The increased pressure destroys the light receptors in the eye. Because glaucoma causes no symptoms, your ophthalmologist detects it by measuring the pressure inside of your eye with a simple, painless procedure during your biannual visit. Treatment usually consists of eye drops two to four times per day. Surgery or laser treatment are options in some cases.

Diabetic Retinopathy

Diabetics whose blood sugar is under poor control are at risk for serious eye problems. These include cataracts, glaucoma, intermittent cloudy vision, and most importantly, changes in retinal blood vessels. The blood vessels in the retina deteriorate and leak plasma or blood, or they may become enlarged enough to interfere with vision.

Sixty percent of quilters who have had diabetes for 15 years will have measurable blood vessel damage to their retinas. Quilters who developed diabetes in childhood are particularly vulnerable. A small number of quilters with diabetic retinopathy will go on to have serious vision problems. Laser surgery can arrest or reverse diabetic retinopathy, and can sometimes restore sight.

If you are diabetic, you must do two things to preserve your vision:
- Keep your blood sugars under control
- Have regular eye exams

Further Reading: Your library will have many books on the eyes. To find them look under these subject words: **vision, eyes, eyestrain, computer eyestrain,** and **eyeglasses.**

THE QUILTER IN THIS CHAPTER
Bertha Mallard (page 44) has been quilting for three years. She recently retired from the Social Security Administration after 30 years of service. She has one son and a granddaughter.

Elizabeth Murray (right) relaxes into the quilt she is making for her baby.

Special Times in a Woman's Life

6 Premenstrual Syndrome & the Quilter

The hormonal shifts that occur during your premenstrual days can take a toll on quiltmaking. This chapter will discuss some of these effects and the ways that you can limit them.

If you are between the ages of 12 and 55, there is an 80% chance you will have some of the following symptoms during the week before your menstrual period.

Aesthetic Problems

When you are undergoing a hormonal shift, you may experience changes in your normal aesthetic abilities. These changes can profoundly affect your quiltmaking, especially if you are designing your quilt or selecting fabric. These changes include:

- Decreased color sense
- Decreased ability to judge shapes and sizes
- Lessened ability to experience creative inspiration
- Markedly altered sense of what is pleasing to your eye

Vision Problems

You may experience a decline in the sharpness of your vision. This can cause eye fatigue and can make it hard to:

- Cut templates accurately
- Cut patches for piecing or appliqué

Hand Problems

Your hands may be swollen and clumsy due to fluid retention. You may experience:

- Decreased manual dexterity
- Decreased eye-hand coordination
- Increased tendency to drop things
- Increased number of skin cuts

Mental Functioning

You have a 70% chance of sleep disturbance in the week before your period. This can lead to generalized brain fuzziness and in turn to:

- Decreased concentration and alertness
- Increased errors in judgment
- Indecisiveness and hesitation
- Decline in your memory
- Decreased ability to reason

Mood Changes

The mood changes of PMS may affect your quiltmaking. They include:

- Irritability and impatience
- A feeling of urgency
- Pessimism

Productivity

The symptoms above can result in a decrease in productivity of 25% on PMS days.

✓**SOLUTIONS** There are many things you can do to limit the effects of your hormonal swings.

Be Aware

Keep track of your menstrual cycle. Mark your likely PMS days on your calendar. Plan quiltmaking activities that are compatible with PMS. Use your PMS days to schedule tasks such as:

- Hand or machine piecing of previously cut patches
- Hand or machine quilting on a previously marked quilt
- Binding a quilt with previously cut binding

Avoid these activities if you have PMS:

- Design work
- Cutting out patches
- Quilt problem solving
- Selecting fabric
- Cutting the binding

Nutrition

What you eat on PMS days will influence how you feel.

- Eat lots of fresh fruit and vegetables.
- Limit the amount of animal protein you consume.
- Avoid salty foods, sugar, caffeine, and alcohol.
- Take a multivitamin with minerals.
- Drink eight glasses of water. This will decrease the amount of fluid you retain.

Plan Ahead

Freeze meals ahead of time to thaw and serve on PMS days.

Elise and Garrett catch forty winks.

Rest

Combat the fatigue and mental fuzziness of PMS with extra nighttime sleep or a daytime nap.

Take Breaks

Breaks are very important on PMS days. Take two 10-minute breaks every hour. During your breaks release tension by stretching like a cat.

Exercise

Gentle exercise such as walking does wonders for your PMS symptoms. Walking for just 6 minutes floods your body with nature's mood elevators, the endorphins. You can walk inside your house or stroll around the block.

Medication

The suggestions within this chapter should provide relief for most quiltmakers with PMS. If you need more help than you have found here, please consult your personal physician.

PMS and Fabric Shopping

Avoid buying fabric on PMS days. Your sense of what is beautiful will likely be altered. The fabric you buy will likely not appeal to you later.

Further Reading: Your public library has many helpful books. Find them by using these subject words: **PMS** and **premenstrual syndrome**.

THE QUILTER IN THIS CHAPTER
Elise SansSouci (this page) has been a quilter for five years and enjoys appliqué. She is a graduate of Wellesley College and is a mom-at-home with Garrett.

The Pregnant Quilter

7

Pregnancy brings new physical and emotional challenges to quiltmakers. This chapter enumerates those challenges and offers solutions. If anything in this chapter goes contrary to the advice of your personal physician, follow her advice.

Hand Problems

Pregnancy causes your body to retain fluid. This results in these hand problems:
- Stiffness and clumsiness
- Increased tendency to drop things

Other Physical Changes

All of the ligaments in your body soften to prepare your body for delivery. The softening of your ligaments, the fluid retention, and your growing baby can create problems that impact your quiltmaking:
- Carpal tunnel syndrome can worsen (or appear for the first time).
- Back pain can worsen (or appear for the first time).
- Your swollen abdomen can limit your access to your quilting hoop, quilt frame, or sewing machine.

Mental Functioning

Eighty percent of pregnant women report disturbed sleep. This, plus hormonal changes and fluid retention lead to:
- Fatigue
- Memory problems
- Decreased concentration and alertness
- Decreased ability to reason

Mood Changes

Some of the mood changes of pregnancy are wonderful. You will experience periods of elation and a new sense of calm. Other mood changes pose challenges to quiltmaking:
- Weepiness
- Oversensitivity
- Fear
- Irritability
- Anxiety

✓ **SOLUTIONS** There are many things you can do to cope with these challenges:

Be Aware

A comprehensive book on pregnancy can provide you with information and reassurance about the physical and mental changes you can expect in each month of your pregnancy.

Your Hands

You can reduce the swelling in your hands safely and easily.

- Fill a dishpan with warm soapy water. Hold a sponge in each hand and squeeze the sponges repeatedly until your fingers limber up. Repeat during your breaks.
- Drink eight glasses of water each day. This will help to reduce swelling throughout your body.

Your Legs

The foot and ankle swelling of pregnancy are uncomfortable. To limit the swelling:

- Avoid crossing your legs when you sit to quilt.
- Take frequent breaks and walk around.
- Drink eight glasses of water a day to help reduce swelling throughout your body.

Your Back

Lower back pain can interfere with quiltmaking. Your softened ligaments and stretched-out abdominal muscles can allow your vertebrae to move out of place. The vertebrae then pinch your nerves and cause pain. There are two things you can do to lessen your chance of developing back pain:

- Maintain good posture. Keep your head, shoulders, and hips in a straight line.
- Try the exercises in Chapter 1 on pages 18 to 21 to strengthen the muscles of your abdomen and back. Ask your doctor if it is okay to do these exercises before you begin. She will likely be pleased to give her blessing.

Your Abdomen

As your baby grows, you may have trouble using your quilting hoop or reaching your sewing machine.

- Try quilting without a hoop or frame. Just hold the quilt in your hands.
- If you must sit farther from your machine than usual, take frequent breaks to rest your arms.

Mental and Emotional Changes

Your fine mind and disposition will return soon after your baby arrives. Meanwhile:

- Avoid caffeine. You will feel more relaxed and mellow.
- Eat frequent healthful snacks to keep your brain well supplied with nutrients.
- Use Post-Its® and lists to help you with memory problems.
- Allow 25% more time for each step of quiltmaking.
- Keep your sense of humor. Pregnancy is a time-limited experience.

Rest

Taking a nap or lying down for 10 minutes will do wonders for your mental functioning and your mood. Rest several times a day if you can.

Take Breaks

Your breaks become especially important now. Take two 10-minute breaks every hour. There are several reasons for this.

- Your needs for rest are increased because of the physical and mental energy consumed by your pregnancy.
- Your ligaments are lax and cannot take the same stresses they can in their normal state.
- The swelling in your hands and wrists makes them more vulnerable to injury.

Exercise

Gentle exercise such as walking will have positive effects on your quiltmaking. Mild exercise will:

- Improve your mood
- Give you more energy
- Decrease swelling throughout your body
- Decrease the discomfort you feel

Women who engage in mild exercise such as walking usually have shorter labors, less fetal distress, and less weight gain in their third trimesters. Check with your doctor before you begin any exercise program. She will probably be delighted that you want to walk.

If Your Due Date is Approaching and Your Baby Quilt is Not Finished

One of the following options will give you a usable baby quilt:
- Quilt it in a few strategic places, then bind it. Keep quilting on it until you deliver.
- Tie it and bind it. Quilt it later, and clip out the ties.
- Utility quilt it and bind it. You can probably complete the quilting in two hours.

Quilting After the Baby Comes

Every pregnant woman dreams of all the things she will accomplish after her baby comes. Dream, but remember that fatigue and sleeplessness will be your way of life for a while. You may be limited to 10-minute blocks of quiltmaking while your baby is small. Plan accordingly:
- Set small, manageable quiltmaking goals for the first few months.
- If you have time before you deliver, make up packets of handwork for your post-baby 10-minute blocks of time.

Further Reading: What to Expect When You Are Expecting by Arlene Eisenberg is an excellent resource. For other titles, look under **pregnancy** in your library's subject catalog.

THE QUILTER IN THIS CHAPTER
Elizabeth Murray (page 54) has been quilting for two years. She is a graduate of Baylor University and is a mom-at-home with Joseph. Until his birth, Elizabeth worked as an executive secretary.

Quiltmaking in the Perimenopause

8

The perimenopause is a 2- to 10-year transition into menopause that most quiltmakers will take. The hormonal shifts of the perimenopause are profound. These shifts are confounding because their timing is irregular and unpredictable.

Your perimenopause will hold challenges for you as a quilter. This chapter discusses many simple things you can do to lessen the impact of hormone fluctuations on your quiltmaking.

Normal Menopause

If you are like most quilters, you will undergo menopause naturally. Your perimenopause may begin anywhere between ages 45 and 55.

Surgical Menopause

Surgical menopause occurs when your ovaries are removed during a surgical procedure. This causes exaggerated symptoms because of the sudden and complete absence of female hormones. A chemical menopause, induced by estrogen-blocking drugs, causes similar exaggerated symptoms.

Premature Menopause

Premature menopause is a condition where your menopause begins in your late thirties or early forties. This occurs in 1% of quilters and is similar to natural menopause.

Eighty-five percent of quiltmakers will experience some of the following symptoms listed during their perimenopause. Twenty percent will experience severe symptoms. The following list includes only the symptoms that can interfere with quiltmaking.

Aesthetic Sense

The hormonal shifts of the perimenopause can have serious effects on your artistic sense. You may experience the following symptoms on an intermittent basis:
- Change in your color sense
- Decreased ability to judge shapes and colors
- Lessened creative inspiration

Mental Functioning

Hormonal shifts at night and the hot flashes they can spawn cause sleeplessness and profound mental and physical fatigue. This fatigue is reminiscent of the fatigue of the first trimester of pregnancy. The loss of sleep can leave you with "mental static" and lead to mental sluggishness and memory problems.

Mood Changes

The mood changes of the perimenopause can be severe. Even quilters who have always been on an even keel experience mood swings that astonish them. The following symptoms can interfere with quiltmaking: irritability, pessimism, a sense of urgency, and depression.

Joint Pain

Your joints can be affected by hormone fluctuations; you may experience shoulder and hip pain.

Hot Flashes

The sense of internal heat, and sometimes even panic, might force you to stop your quiltmaking activities for several minutes at a time.

✓ **SOLUTIONS** There are many things you can do to lessen these symptoms.

Be Aware

Learn all you can about the perimenopause. Always remember the perimenopause is a temporary experience. What lies beyond it is a time of life filled with a zest for living, incredible productivity, and compassion.

Lighting

You now need 50% more light. Use extra lamps and task lighting. Wear your glasses when you stitch.

Rest

Your frequent nighttime awakenings will mean you will need more rest. The stress of coping with your hormone swings will leave you with a great need for rest and relaxation to return you to your normal state:

- Schedule an extra hour of nighttime sleep
- Schedule short naps
- Take a hot bath
- Take a walk
- Be alone for a while
- Treat yourself with respect and kindness

These techniques will actually change your brain waves and "reset" your body to a normal state.

Exercise

Exercise will do wonders for you. Six minutes of gentle walking will release a flood of the body's natural misery-killers, the endorphins. It will also improve your sleep and help regularize your hormones.

Breaks

Take two 10-minute breaks per hour when you are having a "bad hormone day." Stretch.

Joint Pain

Exercise is important in dealing with the joint pain of this time of life. Many quilters develop "frozen" shoulders from disuse due to the pain. If your shoulders or hips begin to ache:

- Keep moving. Move your sore joints through their normal range of movement every day. See the tip on page 25 for an easy way to do this.
- Have a massage focusing on the sore joints

Nutrition

What you eat and drink can influence what you feel:

SUGAR & CAFFEINE Decrease your sugar and caffeine intake, this will smooth out mood swings and lessen hot flashes.

SOYMILK Soymilk contains estrogen-like plant compounds. Keep single-serving boxes of soymilk in your sewing room for "bad hormone days." If mood swings or hot flashes are interfering with your quiltmaking, drink a box of soymilk and walk around the house. You will probably feel better within 5 minutes.

VITAMINS Take a multivitamin with minerals every day to help reduce the symptoms of the perimenopause.

Memory Aids

Make lists. Use Post-Its to help jog your memory. Check your quilt math twice.

Aesthetics

If you sense you are in a hormone fluctuation, avoid buying fabric for a big project. If you have reserved time to select fabric on a hormonally influenced day, buy fat quarters and live with them for a few days to give yourself time to see if you really like them.

Further Reading: I recommend *The Pause: Positive Approaches to Menopause* by Lonnie Barbach. Your library will have this and other titles under the subject indexes of **menopause** and **middle-aged women**.

THE QUILTER IN THIS CHAPTER
Jan Gadberry (pages 58–59) has been a quilter for 17 years. She is the mother of two grown children and has one grandchild. She owns Silver Threads Quilt Shop in Plano, Texas.

The Golden Years of Quiltmaking

9

Your golden years bring you the time to make the quilts you have always dreamed of. These years also bring challenges. This chapter discusses age-related changes that can affect quiltmaking and shows you how you can stay in peak physical and mental condition.

Vision

Ninety percent of quilters over the age of 65 require corrective eyeglasses because of changes in the lenses inside their eyes. Other eye problems can affect quiltmaking also:
- **Cataracts:** Cataracts occur when the lens inside the eye becomes cloudy.
  - 15% of 65-year-old quilters have cataracts
  - 40% of 75-year-old quilters have them
- **Macular Degeneration:** This is a decline in the area of the retina that has the sharpest vision. It occurs in:
  - 5% of 65-year-old quiltmakers
  - 20% of 75-year-old quilters
- **Dry Eyes:** Older eyes are drier. This can cause discomfort when you use your eyes continuously as you do in quiltmaking.
- **Light Requirements:** Mature eyes require 70% more light than young eyes.
- **Color Sense:** Mature eyes have trouble distinguishing between like colors. This is because the lens of the eye has become yellowed.
- **Contrast Problems:** Changes in the nerve cells in the back of the eye and the yellowing of the lens make it harder for you to see differences in value between fabrics. You may also experience difficulty seeing your quilting stitches.

Fingers and Hands

Changes in your body and in your immune system can affect quiltmaking:
- The pads of your finger are 20% thinner. Needle pricks can do more damage to your finger pads.
- Your skin is drier and more fragile.
- Injuries to your fingers may take four times longer to heal than when you were younger.
- Your white cells do not fight infection as well. This means you are more vulnerable to infection where the needle pierces your finger.
- Arthritis may cause morning stiffness in your fingers and hands.

- The cartilage that forms the joints in your fingers and hands is weaker and drier.
- You will be a little clumsier, have a slower reaction time, and have less control of your fingers. This means that fine work will be harder and you will have more cuts and bruises.
- Tremors may make fine hand work difficult.

Memory Problems

Your short-term memory begins its slow decline in your forties. By age 65 this is very noticeable. You may have trouble following the directions in a pattern or sewing blocks together properly.

Mood

Sometimes the decline in functioning that accompanies aging can cause discouragement and depression.

Bones and Joints

The internal structure of your bones is shaped by their use. Inactivity severely weakens your bones. Activity strengthens them.

Medications

Some medications can blur vision. Blood thinners can cause problems when your needle pricks your finger.

✓**SOLUTIONS** There are many things you can do to cope with these changes.

Eyes and Lighting

A yearly checkup can help you to keep your vision at its peak. Your eye doctor will check you for cataracts and evaluate you for macular degeneration. She can update your prescription and offer you personalized advice for overcoming any vision problems you are encountering in quiltmaking. Wearing your glasses when you sew is very important.

Sufficient light is imperative. You must arrange your lighting so you have bright, glare-free, shadow-free lighting. You may need a lamp on each side of your sewing chair. A stronger light is always worth more than a stronger prescription.

BLINKING If you blink every 30 seconds you will be able to keep your eyes moist and comfortable. Practice this for 5 minutes while watching a clock with a sweep second hand. Drink eight glasses of water a day. If these don't do the trick, call your eye doctor for her recommendations for moisturizing eye drops. Avoid allergy-type eye drops. These worsen eye dryness.

CONTRAST PROBLEMS If you are having trouble distinguishing between fabrics, use high-contrast fabric combinations such as red and white. Use contrasting quilting thread if you can no longer see your stitches. If using contrasting thread isn't enough, try utility quilting: use #8 perle cotton and a size 5 needle and make small running stitches. You can utility quilt in your hands or use a hoop.

RESOURCES FOR LOW-VISION QUILTERS The Maxi catalog and the Lighthouse catalog have products for low-vision quilters. See Sources (page 111) for how you can obtain these catalogs.

For more on vision see Chapter 5 (page 42).

Fingers and Hands

The maturing process is hard on your fingers and hands. Fortunately, there are many things you can do that will keep you quilting into your nineties.

Needle Pricks

If needle pricks are causing you to have increased finger pain, try using reusable stick-on barrier pads. Choose between soft plastic Thimble-Its and soft leather Thimble-Pads. The pads work like a callus to protect your finger. They are so comfortable you will forget you are wearing them.

If you prefer to work with a bare under-quilt finger, use an antibacterial dishwashing detergent. This will cut down on the number of skin bacteria that your needle can carry into your finger. Massage your sore fingers with your thumb to increase circulation and speed healing.

Dry Skin

Your drier skin will need lotion to keep it soft and healthy.

Arthritis

Arthritis causes pain and morning stiffness. Morning stiffness can be worked out by squeezing two sponges in a pan of warm, soapy water.

- Painkillers can help if your finger joints ache while you quilt. I recommend Tylenol because it doesn't weaken your white cells.
- Some quilters rub an ice-cold soda can over their sore joints during breaks. Others squeeze sponges in a basin of warm water. Do whichever feels best to you.
- If you walk for 30 minutes four times a week, your fingers will become more flexible and your arthritis pain will decrease dramatically. Begin slowly and take two months to build up to this level.

Tremors

Tremors can be a real nuisance to quilters. If tremors are interfering with your quiltmaking, try one of these tips:

- When piecing, try resting your forearms and the sides of your hands on your kitchen table.
- When quilting, brace the heel of your hand against your hoop or against the surface of your quilt.
- If your tremor is severe, utility quilt or tie your quilts.
- Sometimes medication can help with tremors. Discuss this with your doctor.

Sharp Tools

Be a little more careful with needles, scissors, and rotary cutters. Age makes us a bit clumsier and our wounds take four times as long to heal.

For more on the care of your fingers see Chapter 4 (page 35).

Rest

Breaks become very important as you age. Take two 10-minute breaks every hour. Your body needs the rest time to re-lubricate your joints and tendons. Drink eight glasses of water on the days you quilt. This helps lubricate your joints and tendons and helps to plump up your joint cartilage.

Betty Lou pins a sample block on the wall behind her machine to help her remember how it goes together. She has a task light beside her machine.

Memory and Mental Function

Short-term memory problems begin in the forties and persist throughout life.

- Make lists and use Post-Its to help with memory problems.
- Pin a sample block over your machine and refer to it often. This will help you to avoid construction errors and time-consuming rip-outs.
- Walk four days a week. This will improve your memory and your ability to reason.
- Stay connected with people. This will keep your mind sharp. Your quilting group is a perfect place to keep in contact with others.

Mental Attitude and Mood

Almost every quilter becomes discouraged with the aches, pains, and losses of aging. If you experience this, do the following to create a surge of nature's feel-good chemicals, the endorphins:

- Count your blessings
- Laugh

- Commit random acts of kindness
- Serve others
- Walk

If you have a severe depression that does not respond to the above, see your doctor. Severe mood problems may require medication to reverse chemical imbalances in your brain.

Exercise, Your Bones, and Longevity

A gentle exercise program will work miracles on your overall health, well-being, and longevity:
- Quilters who walk 4 times a week for 30 minutes live 3 years longer and delay the onset of the symptoms of old age by 7 years.
- They have fewer hip fractures, fewer heart problems, and less cancer.
- Strong bones come from regular gentle exercise. You can regain your strength and agility no matter what your age.

If you want to live a long and happy life, start walking. See Chapter 14 for more on exercise (page 93).

Nutrition

Eat healthful foods. Take a multivitamin with minerals every day.

Medication

See page 70 for ways to cope with some of the side effects of medication.

THE BOTTOM LINE Diet, exercise, and loving self-care play a huge role in the quality of life you will experience in your golden years.

Further Reading: I recommend *The American Geriatric Society's Complete Guide to Aging and Health* by Dr. Mark Williams. Your library will have a wealth of information on the aging process. Look under the following subject headings: **aging**, **geriatrics**, **old age**, **longevity**, and **degeneration**.

THE QUILTER IN THIS CHAPTER
Betty Lou Wood (pages 62 and 65) has been a quilter for 20 years. She is the mother of four grown children and grandmother of six. A third-generation seamstress, she owns a business specializing in custom wedding gowns and special occasion dresses.

Personal Injury or Illness— Embracing Change

10

Personal injury or illness can put a damper on your quiltmaking activities. So can the use of certain prescription medications. This chapter suggests ways to deal with both.

Personal Injury or Illness

Personal injury or illness may be as simple and time-limited as a broken finger, or as pervasive and ongoing as rheumatoid arthritis.

Maintain a Positive Attitude

This is the single most important thing you can do to speed your recovery. Make maintaining a positive attitude your first priority.

- Begin to count your blessings. Write them down, if possible, or dictate them to a loved one.
- Laugh. Laughter shortens convalescence, especially belly laughs. Humorous books or movies can work wonders to speed your healing.
- Gentle exercise will lift your mood and release natural painkillers and mood-elevators.

Stay Connected with Quiltmaking

Maintain your regular contacts with the world of quiltmaking.

- Attend your quilting small group.
- Attend guild meetings.
- Refill your creative well by reading quiltmaking books and magazines.
- Play with your fabric. Put together new fabric combinations.
- Design a new quilt.

Do Volunteer Work

Volunteer work within the quiltmaking world can put your mind back on a larger universe. Hostess your quilting small group. Or call the volunteer coordinator of your quilt guild and volunteer to:

- Make phone calls
- Organize a new small group
- Help with your guild's new member tea

- Organize a service project
- Help with guild publicity
- Sell raffle tickets for your guild's fund raiser
- Organize a day trip to visit all of the quilt shops in your area
- Hostess a quilting bee to work on your guild's raffle quilt

Injuries to Your Hand, Wrist, or Arm

A broken finger, carpal tunnel syndrome, or a fractured arm may sideline you from quiltmaking. Use the tips above and:
- Get some exercise. It can be as simple as a walk around the block.
- Keep quilts near you. Look at them. Touch them.
- Remain involved with your quiltmaking friends.

Permanent Disability of Your Hands, Wrists, or Arms

Major trauma and computer-related injuries can sometimes produce permanent disability. Try using the machine for piecing, appliqué, and quilting. Also ask your doctor to schedule a consultation with an occupational therapist. She will be able to help you to find ways to continue to make quilts.

Neck Injuries

Cervical neck problems and whiplash injuries can make quiltmaking very difficult. Use the tips above and:
- Be faithful to your rehab exercises.
- Begin a walking program.
- Put your quilts where you will see them every day.
- Stay connected to the world of quiltmaking, even if you cannot stitch right now.

Neck Surgery

If you have had neck surgery, you may not feel mentally able to read, sew, or go to quilt meetings for several weeks. That's perfectly normal. When you are ready, use the tips above to ease back into the quilting world. Meanwhile:
- Keep quilts where you can see and touch them.
- Wrap yourself in a quilt while you rest.

Injuries to Your Feet and Legs

These injuries may limit walking, but usually leave your hands free for quilting. Use the tips on page 67 and above, and:
- Do the exercises in Chapter 1 on pages 18–21. Try holding a soup can in each hand while you do the "shower" exercises.

- Ask your friends for rides to small group and guild so you stay connected with other quilters.
- Use the time to finish projects you started long ago.

Eye Injuries

Eye injuries cause a temporary halt to quiltmaking. Remember:
- If your doctor has prescribed eye rest, *rest your eyes.*
- Exercise by walking, if your doctor allows it.
- Ask for rides to guild and small group.
- Fill your creative well by listening to music.
- Keep quilts near you. Look at them. Touch them.

Eye Disease

Long-term eye problems will require creative approaches to quiltmaking. If there is a will, there is a way:
- Experiment with magnifiers and brighter light.
- Use fabrics with great contrast between them.
- Use contrasting quilting thread.
- Utility quilt with contrasting thread.
- Tie quilts.
- Work with a low-vision specialist. "Adaptive technology" for low vision may offer you the perfect tool you need to keep stitching.

Chronic Illness

A chronic or lengthy illness, such as rheumatoid arthritis, multiple sclerosis, or cancer may interfere with quiltmaking. Chronic or lengthy illness causes pain, fatigue, and malaise. The treatments for your illness may interfere with quiltmaking because they are time consuming or because the treatment causes suffering.

Your world may constrict to include only your sickroom. After your treatment is underway, expand your horizons and reclaim the world of quilting. You became a quilter because quilting is a wonderful stress-reliever. It will be that for you again.

Back pain keeps Ginny from leaning over to assist her students, so she sits beside them.

Try the following things as you reclaim quilting:

- Schedule at least one belly laugh every day.
- Exercise. If you have serious pain or disability, ask your doctor to schedule an appointment with a physical therapist to help you find a way to exercise. Exercise will provide you with natural painkillers and mood-elevators.
- If your disability interferes with quilt-making, ask your doctor to schedule a consultation with an occupational therapist to show you how to keep quilting. You need the natural feel-good chemicals that quiltmaking gives you.
- Volunteer any way you can. Being with people will work wonders for your well-being.

Ginny, who has rheumatoid arthritis, applies a cold pack to her knee while she stitches.

Medication Affecting Quiltmaking

There are three main categories of prescription drugs that affect quiltmaking: drugs that blur vision, blood-thinners, and chemotherapy drugs.

Drugs that Blur Your Vision

Many drugs can blur your vision. Sometimes your doctor can prescribe another drug that will not blur your vision. It is also possible that the drug you are currently taking can be taken on a different schedule that will free up periods of clear vision. Work closely with your doctor to find a solution.

Call your doctor to find out if there is another medication that will treat your symptoms without blurring your vision. If not, proceed as follows:

- Determine what time of day you want to have clear vision for quiltmaking. Make a note of it.
- For the next seven days, record the exact times you take your medication.

- During this seven-day period make careful notes about when you experience blurred vision. Note when it starts and when it begins to clear up.

Now call or visit your doctor. Have your notes in hand.
- Tell her what time of day you want to have clear vision.
- Tell her how soon after a dose your vision blurs and when it starts to improve.
- Ask her if she can adjust your dosage schedule to allow you to have clear vision during the time you have selected for quiltmaking.

Blood-thinners

Anti-coagulants slow the clotting process. This means that every deep needle prick can leave a big drop of blood on the back of your quilt. One way to limit needle pricks is to wear one of the new stick-on needle barriers. Use the soft plastic Thimble-It, the leather Thimble-Pads, or the metal UnderThimble.

These barriers will not prevent all needle pricks. Make a plan now to deal with blood on your quilt. Each of these methods works best when used immediately:
- Use your saliva to remove fresh bloodstains. There is an enzyme in your saliva that will decolorize your blood.
- Use cold water on the bloodstain. Remember that the water may travel to the front of your quilt and remove the markings.
- Use hydrogen peroxide, applied with a Q-tip®. Pretest it on a scrap of every fabric in your quilt, back and front. Also, test it on a scrap containing the marking method you use.

It you are on a blood-thinner and quilt away from home, pack a blood removal kit in your tote.

Chemotherapy

Anti-cancer medications can have a profound effect on quiltmaking. In addition to thinning the finger pads and fingernails, these drugs cause a lowered white cell count and profound tiredness.
- Use an anti-bacterial dishwashing liquid to minimize the number of bacteria on your hands.
- Use a leather thimble on your right needle-pushing finger for piecing and appliqué if your finger pads and nails have thinned, or use a stick-on needle barrier like Thimble-It.
- Use stick-on needle barriers on your left index and middle fingers to prevent needle pricks when you do handwork or quilt.
- Rub Bacitracin ointment into your fingertips after you finish stitching.

- If you have had lymph nodes removed under your arms, and currently have a low white count, ask your doctor if it is safe for you to prick your finger. Tell her which of the measures above you have chosen to protect your fingers.
- Massage your fingertips frequently.
- Get more rest.

Further Reading: Your library will have many books to help you. Use these subject indexes: **illness, disability, disease, wellness, sickness, chronic diseases, adjustment, stress, stress management, wit and humor, laughter, relaxation, peace of mind,** and **women's health and hygiene**.

THE QUILTERS IN THIS CHAPTER

Ginny Kenney (pages 69–70) has been quilting for 20 years. She founded the Quilter's Guild of Plano, Texas. Ginny has raised two children and teaches bear-making at quilt shops.

Ginny's student Debbie Campbell (page 69) is a mom-at-home to Erin. She is past-President of the Quilter's Guild of Plano and works at Silver Threads Quilt Shop.

Julie Flemming (right) wraps herself in her childhood quilt every morning and goes over her family's schedule for the day. She works part time as a geophysicist and serves on the Board of her children's school. Her co-workers, fellow quilters, and board members tease her about her packet of index cards, but she would be lost without them.

Time Management & Health

11 How to Make Time to Quilt

Quiltmaking melts away the stresses of your day. It also brings incredible health benefits. Quiltmaking:

- Reduces your heart rate
- Drops your blood pressure
- Produces relaxation throughout your body
- Improves the quality of your sleep
- Helps protect you from colds and flu
- Improves your body's ability to heal injuries

Quiltmaking's quiet pace keeps you in touch with your inner wisdom so you can make good life choices.

You are given 168 hours every week. Choose the ways you will invest this bounty of time. Always schedule time for the things that are genuinely important to you.

If you would like to have more time for quiltmaking, take the time now for a time-management makeover.

Your Time-Management Makeover

Grab your family calendar and look at your schedule for the upcoming seven days. Note your plans and responsibilities in the following categories:

Self-Care

This is the most important category. Unless you care for yourself, you will not be able to care for anyone else. How much time do you allot for:

- Sleeping
- Everyday grooming
- Eating
- Exercise
- One-on-one contact with your friends
- Phone calls to maintain your support system
- Letters or e-mail to distant friends
- Club meetings, including quilt guild
- Reading, including reading about quiltmaking
- Church or temple, classes, and Scripture study
- Weekly day of rest and spiritual refreshment
- Focused, at home quiltmaking

Care of Your Family

Providing a loving, nurturing environment and delicious, nourishing meals is probably a big priority for you. How much time do you allot for marriage maintenance, care and feeding of your family, housework, carpools, elder-care, and volunteer work?

Employment

Are you a quiltmaker who contributes to your family's income? How much time do you allot for your employment-related activities?

- Hours of work per week
- Daily commute time
- Travel
- Work-related reading
- Continuing education workshops
- Work completed at home

Slack

Do you build slack into your schedule to allow for the unexpected? How much time do you allow for:

- Illnesses
- Appliance repairs
- Other unplanned demands on your time

If you build in slack for the inevitable emergencies of life, you will not have to surrender your precious quiltmaking time to deal with the urgent situations that arise.

Tallying the Results

Add up the total number of hours you have committed for the next seven days. Compare your total to the 168 hours available to you. If you have less than 168 hours in your schedule, it will be a simple matter for you to schedule more quiltmaking time. If you have more than 168 hours planned, you must examine your priorities carefully.

Setting Priorities

You will rely on your deepest and truest wisdom as you determine what in your current schedule is truly important to you. Your values will be a little bit different than those of any other quilter.

Go through the list you just made. Take a hard look at your commitments.

Your Responsibilities to Yourself

Look at your responsibilities to yourself first of all. Do not skimp on the time necessary to care for yourself. There is nothing selfish about self-care.

Now determine how many hours per week you would like to devote to focused, at-home quiltmaking time. Focused time is time when you have minimal other demands on you. You will use focused time for:

- Designing your quilts
- Selecting the fabric for your quilts
- Solving the problems that arise as your quilts evolve
- Preparing handwork for your "found" quilting time

Write down the number of hours you wish to spend each week on focused quilting time. Later in this chapter we will talk about finding and using small blocks of time for your prepared handwork.

Your Responsibilities to Your Family

You take your responsibilities to your family very seriously. Examine the time you spend in direct service to your family. Are you spending enough time with each family member? Too much time? If you need to make a correction, write that down.

Now look at the time you spend meeting the physical needs of your family. Try the following to free up time for quiltmaking.

Shop smarter. Save up your errands and do them all on one day. Run your errands during slow periods in the stores. Limit unscheduled trips to the store by stockpiling:

- Personal care items
- School supplies, including poster board
- The ingredients for several quick meals

Look at the volunteer work you do at your children's schools and in the community. Are you doing too much? If you need to make a change, write it down.

Your Work Responsibilities

Examine the demands your work makes on you. Are you doing too much? If you need to make a change, make a note.

Putting It All Together

Go over your list again. You will probably experience discomfort when you think about dropping some of your activities. This is normal.

Think about your list during quiet moments in the shower. Consider it at stoplights. Ponder it while you quilt. Instead of the panic you felt when you first considered change, you will begin to feel a quiet assurance about what must change. Your own inner wisdom will reveal to you the right way to apportion your 168 hours.

Rework your schedule according to your clarified priorities. Plan your focused quilting time for your most productive hours, if possible. Write your focused quilting time on your calendar in ink.

"Found" Focused Time

Sometimes circumstances arise that present you with "free" focused quilting time. Seize these times for quiltmaking: if your husband or kids are away or if you are traveling alone. Take advantage of time when other family members are sleeping.

"Buy" focused quilting time by cooking double batches of stews and casseroles and freezing half. When you need an extra hour for focused quiltmaking, pull out the frozen meal.

Julie pieces in her doctor's waiting room. She carries her supplies in a red plastic pencil case.

"Found" Quilting Time

Prepare handwork during your focused quilting time and have it ready to go. You will discover you have many small blocks of quilting time. Using these blocks of time could give you several hours more of quiltmaking time every week. If you have switched to machine quiltmaking because of time pressure, you can rediscover the health-giving rhythms of handwork. You can find quiltmaking time in the following situations:

- Doctor's appointments
- TV watching time
- Break time at work
- The pick-up line at school
- Car trips or other travel
- Committee meetings

Keep a tote packed with the supplies you need for your current project. Keep it with you in the kitchen, family room, car, and whenever you have sit-down time away from home. Carry only what you need.

Further Reading: Your library will have many books on **time management**. The following titles offer good suggestions for family time management:

The Family Manager's Everyday Survival Guide by Kathy Peel

Time Management for Busy People by Roberta Roesch

THE QUILTER IN THIS CHAPTER

Julie Flemming (this page) has been quilting for four years. As a mother and part-time geophysicist, she relies on a combination of focused quilting time and found time to produce two to three quilts every year.

12 Stress-free Quiltmaking

Quiltmaking is very good for you. It melts away the stresses of your day, improves your sleep, and helps your body fight infection. In order to reap these important health benefits, you must create peaceful and ordered time in which to create your quilts. Cultivate these virtues:

- Honestly estimating the time needed to make your quilt
- Allowing extra time for the quiltmaking steps that are especially pleasurable for you
- Allowing extra time for the parts of quiltmaking that are distasteful to you

This chapter will help you gain the skills you need for stress-free quiltmaking.

Learning to Estimate the Time You Will Need to Complete Your Quilt

You will need a spiral notebook or a loose-leaf binder. You will use this to:

- Record your estimates about how long each step of the quiltmaking process will take.
- Make daily notes about the process, including the actual time that each step required.

Allow a separate page for each of the following steps listed. If your quilt requires steps not listed here, include pages for them, also.

1. Design
2. Quilt math
3. Accumulating fabric
4. Washing and ironing
5. Marking and cutting
6. Organizing patches and appliqué into portable units for handwork
7. Organizing patches and appliqué for machine work
8. Piecing or appliquéing your blocks
9. Pressing your blocks
10. Setting your blocks and creating borders
11. Pressing your quilt top
12. Marking your top for quilting
13. Washing, ironing, and seaming the fabric for the quilt back

14. Layering and basting
15. Quilting
16. Washing and ironing the binding fabric; cutting and pressing the strips of binding
17. Applying the binding
18. Removing the markings and washing your quilt
19. Adding a sleeve for shows

Placing Your Time Estimate in the Context of Your Life

After you have made a preliminary estimate of the time it will take to create your quilt, pull out this year's calendar and last year's. Ask yourself the following questions:
- What holidays, anniversaries, and family birthdays are coming up?
- What time commitments did you encounter last year in these months?
- Do you have health care issues that will require you to take more time for rest and breaks when you make this quilt?

Now look at the weeks and months ahead. What potential "found" time can you anticipate: car trips, committee meetings, late night or early morning when the house is quiet. Can you carve out other special times to work on your quilt?

A Real-World Time Estimate

Now put it all together. Modify your preliminary estimate:
- Identify the steps in the quiltmaking process you want to savor. Add 25% to your time estimate for those individual steps.
- Identify the steps in the process that are hard for you. Add 25% to your time estimate for those steps.
- Make a new total.
- Add 10% for unforeseen emergencies.
- Record your final estimate in your notebook.
- Examine your estimate in the light of your deadline and the commitments you discovered when you reviewed your calendars. Examine it in the light of any large blocks of "found time" you identified.

While You Are Working on Your Quilt

Make notes every day you work on the quilt. Note times when you had planned to work on your quilt but couldn't.

When you have finished your quilt, you will have a real-world journal of what your personal quiltmaking life is like. This will help you to make a good estimate of how long it will take you to make your next quilt. This way, quiltmaking will always be a stress-free, life-giving part of your life.

Elise SansSouci (right) lost 15 pounds last year by simply walking every day pushing Garrett's stroller.

Nutrition & Exercise

13 What Do You Have to Lose?

Weight control is the number one health care concern of quiltmakers. In this chapter, I will show you how to create a lifelong eating plan. If you embrace this plan, you will never have to diet again. Your extra pounds will slowly melt away.

Your eating plan will consist of:

- Foods that are bursting with flavor
- Foods you love
- Foods that will love you back

I will show you real-world strategies for healthy, soul-nourishing eating when you are at home, at the office, or traveling. I will offer tips on making healthy choices in fast-food restaurants, in other restaurants, and during the holidays.

Your eating plan will include:

- Modest amounts of every food you love
- A moderate amount of fat
- Healthy, satisfying portions of meat and fish
- Plentiful quantities of flavor-packed grains
- Bountiful fresh, seasonal fruits and vegetables
- Sensible amounts of sugar

You will have a new focus on what you should be eating and a much smaller focus on what you shouldn't.

The health benefits of this plan are abundant. In addition to weight loss, your lifelong meal-planning strategy will reduce your risk of:

- Heart disease
- Diabetes
- Osteoporosis
- High blood cholesterol
- Cancer
- Stroke
- High blood pressure

Why Change Your Way of Eating?

Two thirds of Americans are overweight, including many quilters. Why are Americans, and quiltmakers in particular, so prone to being overweight?

The answer to this question is very complex. There are at least thirteen factors that influence weight gain in quiltmakers. I will give you an overview of these issues, then discuss each in detail.

Why are Americans Overweight?

- We sit for long periods and seldom exercise
- Our past diets have robbed us of fat-burning muscle
- We eat more fat than our bodies need
- We eat too much sugar and too much processed grain
- We don't eat enough fiber
- We do not drink enough water to allow our bodies to burn fat
- We do not eat enough fresh, seasonal fruits and vegetables
- Retailers tempt us with super-sized food items
- We skip breakfast
- We buy fast, soul-less food
- We eat when we are not hungry
- We eat too much when we dine out
- We gain 7 pounds, on the average, every December

Let's look at these problem areas, one by one. Make a note of the ones that apply to you. After you finish reading this chapter, reread the sections that apply to you. Pick one area you would like to work on. Work on that area until you have integrated the change into your lifestyle. Then you can pick another area to tackle. If your doctor has prescribed an eating plan for you that is different than this one, discuss any changes you want to make with her.

The eating plan I will outline is not a fad diet. It is an eating plan for your whole life. This plan will nourish every layer of your being, your body, your mind, and your soul.

Our Sedentary Lifestyle

We quiltmakers sit for long periods of time. Our natures demand it. Our craft requires it. When you sit for long hours two things happen:

- Your metabolism slows down. This means your body begins to burn fewer calories every minute. If you sit and quilt for one hour, your metabolism drops by 15%.
- Your muscles begin to shrink. The average quilter loses 10 pounds of muscle between ages 20 and 40. This muscle loss is due to disuse. This loss of muscle is very important because muscles burn fat.

The slowdown in metabolic rate and the muscle loss are a prescription for weight gain.

✓**SOLUTIONS** The solution is simple. You have to get moving.

- Take a break for 10 minutes every hour. Stretch, visit the rest room, and drink a glass of water. Then "rev up" your metabolism by walking inside your house for 6 minutes. Make circuits through your kitchen, dining room, and family room.
- You can regain your normal, feminine muscles no matter what your age. The next chapter shows you how you can do this by using skills you already have. You won't have to spend a single penny.

Past Diets

Calorie restricting diets cause you to burn fat and muscle in almost equal pro-portions. If you lose 11 pounds on a calorie restricting diet, you will lose 5 pounds of fat and 6 pounds of muscle. The loss of 6 pounds of muscle dra-matically lowers your body's ability to burn calories. That's why the weight comes right back, plus bonus weight you never had before. Calorie restricting diets have another drawback. They inspire binge-eating. Because your body thinks it is starving, it will store every calorie in your binge as fat.

✓**SOLUTIONS**

- Rebuild your lost muscle by gentle, enjoyable exercise—like walking. The next chapter will help you do this.
- Never calorie restrict. Instead, learn to eat delicious, soul-satisfying, health-giving meals and snacks that are packed with fresh fruits and vegetables, whole grains, and modest portions of meats and desserts.

Our Fat Intake

Fat is a very important part of a healthy diet. You need fat to make hormones and to keep your digestion running smoothly.

✓**SOLUTIONS**

- If you want to regain your girlish figure, you must make a modest cutback in your fat intake. By modest, I mean to cut your fat intake back by one third. To do this, take a hard look at the sources of fat in your diet. Choose lean cuts of meat. Cut back on your intake of butter, oil, and fried foods. Do not eliminate these foods from your diet. Just cut back.
- Add abundant quantities of healthful, nutrient-packed fruits and vegetables to your diet. These foods have the flavor, crunch, and bulk that turn off hunger. If you eat nine servings of fresh fruit and vegetables every day, you will automatically eat less fat.

- Eat modest portions of your favorite foods such as fried chicken or lasagna. Have these favorites once a month. On days you eat your beloved high-fat foods, choose a low-fat lunch or supper.
- Become a french-fry moocher. Take three french fries from a friend's order.
- Try the lower-fat dairy products. Choose the lowest fat ones that still taste delicious to you.
- Avoid sugary "non-fat" or "low-fat" foods.

Sugar and Highly Processed Grains

We have developed a taste for sugar and for processed grains.
- In 1900 the average quilter ate 7 pounds of sugar a year.
- Today we eat 126 pounds of sugar a year.

Our bodies are not equipped to handle this much sugar. Our bodies secrete massive amounts of insulin in response to the overdose of sugar. The insulin forces your body to store the sugar as fat. That's why "fat-free" cookies end up on your thighs the next morning. The over-secretion of insulin from eating sugar does more than build fat. It causes profound hunger 90 minutes later. This means that we eat again. These extra calories mean more weight gain.

Artificial sweeteners are not a solution. They also cause over-secretion of insulin. People who drink diet drinks gain more weight than people who drink regular soda. Artificial sweeteners have another downside. They accustom you to extreme sweetness. This means naturally delicious foods such as fresh fruit do not taste sweet to you.

In 1900, quilters ate whole grains. They saved white flour for "feast" days. Today we eat white flour every day. White flour causes more insulin secretion than whole-wheat flour. The white flour ends up on your thighs as fat.

✓SOLUTIONS
- Notice how much sugar you are eating. Cut back to 7 teaspoons a day.
- Explore the sources of whole grains. Try whole grain breads and pastas. King Arthur® White Whole Wheat flour is a mild whole-wheat flour that even kids will eat.
- Avoid commercial "fat-free" treats.
- Treat sugary foods as "luxury" foods. Enjoy them on special occasion days. Eat them in small quantities on non-feast-days. Eat sugary foods with great ceremony. Take small bites. Taste every single calorie.

Fiber

Most quilters do not get enough fiber in their diets. Enough is 25 grams per day. Fiber has three important weight loss benefits:

- Eating a high-fiber diet gives you a 10% discount on the calories you consume. Ten percent of the calories you eat stay in your bowel, stuck to the fiber. These calories are excreted naturally.
- Fiber gives you a sense of having eaten plenty of food, so you stop eating sooner.
- The extra chewing that fiber requires also works to turn off hunger.

✓SOLUTIONS

- Eat whole grain foods, such as whole wheat, oatmeal, or brown rice.
- Eat loads of fresh fruits and vegetables—nine half-cup servings every day.
- Eat plenty of beans.
- Eat bread or cereal with added bran.
- When you bake, use whole grain flours in dark or highly seasoned baked goods. Your family will never know.

Water

Your body needs abundant quantities of water to complete the chemical reaction that burns fat. Drink eight glasses of water a day.

Drink an 8-ounce glass of water right now. The water will:

- Boost your energy level by 10%
- Reduce any hunger you may be feeling
- Increase your metabolism
- Allow your body to burn fat
- Force you to take a break in one hour
- Improve the functioning of your eyes, fingers, wrists, muscles and intervertebral disks

✓SOLUTIONS

Drink a glass of water during your break or sip water while you quilt, and vary the water you choose:

- Tap water
- Plain spring water
- Sparkling water
- Flavored, unsweetened sparkling water
- Very hot water
- Ice water

The Absence of Fresh, Seasonal Fruits and Vegetables in Our Diet

Juicy ripe fruits and vegetables are extremely soul-satisfying. Our bodies crave precisely the fruits and vegetables that are coming to harvest in the season we are in.

Eating foods made with fresh, seasonal vegetables provides abundant flavor, deep satisfaction, and loads of fiber. Nutritionists say if they can convince people to eat nine servings of fresh or steamed fruits and vegetables every day, weight melts off of them. People who eat fresh or steamed fruits and vegetables in these quantities automatically eat less fat because they feel so full and satisfied.

✓ SOLUTIONS

- Get back in touch with what fruits and vegetables are coming to harvest in each season.
- If it looks good, buy it. One of your cookbooks will have a perfect recipe.
- Let today's super-sized fruit work for you. Eat a large apple, a large orange, or a large banana and you've eaten two servings of fruit.
- Bake an extra white or sweet potato when you make supper and have it for lunch tomorrow. A medium-sized russet potato is two servings. ·
- Prepare a double batch of steamed vegetables when you make supper and have the extra with your lunch tomorrow.

Super-sizing

A "serving" of food is one half-cup. Food retailers offer super-sized foods that are two, three, and four times this size. If you eat most super-sized foods you will add unwanted pounds.

- An average restaurant meal contains more than half your day's calories. That's *without* an appetizer or dessert. Fast food meals can have a similar calorie count.
- Super-sized soft drinks can contain 800 calories.

The only super-sized foods that are "good values" are fresh fruits and vegetables.

✓ SOLUTIONS

- Over the next week, keep a half-cup measure with you at all times. When you are at home, measure everything you eat. When you eat away from home, set your measuring cup on the table beside you and visually estimate the number of half-cup servings in your food. You will quickly learn to judge serving sizes.

- In restaurants, if you are served more food than you planned to eat, ask for a to-go container.
- If you are dining with a friend, split an entrée. The extra plate charge will seem insignificant the next day when you notice you haven't gained weight.

Breakfast

Eating breakfast satisfies your body's needs for fuel and sets your body's metabolic furnace on high. If you skip this meal, two things will happen:

- You will overeat at lunch and dinner to meet your body's demand for fuel
- More of the calories you eat will turn to fat

✓ SOLUTION

- Chose a well-balanced, high-protein breakfast. Plan to eat at least 500 calories at breakfast.

Eating Soul-less Food

Every single bite of food you eat should nourish your body, your mind, and your soul. If it doesn't, you will search for the missing "nourishment" in non-hunger eating.

When you eat, do not do anything else. Do not quilt, use the phone, type, or drive. If you choose a drive-through meal, park your car under a beautiful tree while you eat.

The aroma, beauty, texture, and flavor of foods all satisfy hunger and add to your feeling of fullness. Indulge in these natural hunger stoppers:

- Stop to appreciate the beauty and aroma of your food before you take a single bite.
- Take one bite. Note the temperature of your food and how the temperature enhances the flavor.
- Notice the texture of the food. Enjoy the mouth-feel of every bite.
- Put down your fork while you chew. If you are holding your food, rest your wrist on the table.
- Take small bites. Taste every single calorie.

Presentation and ceremony will also add to your sense of fullness. Try these ideas:

- If possible, light a votive candle while you eat your lunch at your desk. If you are dining at home, light a regular candle.
- Use a lovely plate for your snacks. If you are eating an apple, slice it into wedges, arrange them on the plate and add a small handful of walnuts.
- Carry a tape of exquisite, soul-filled music in your car. Play it while you sit under a graceful tree to eat your lunch.

Non-hunger Eating

Physical discomfort and emotional discomfort can lead to non-hunger eating. Physical causes of non-hunger eating include:

- Muscle tension from coffee, black tea, or hot chocolate; a lack of breaks; and a lack of careful stretching during breaks
- Pain from poor posture
- Muscle strain resulting from poor muscle tone
- Discomfort resulting from ill-fitting seating, inadequate task lighting, and uncomfortable room temperature

✓ SOLUTIONS

- Limit tension-causing beverages such as coffee, black tea, or hot chocolate.
- Begin your hourly breaks with stretching (see page 15).
- Sit in good posture, with your head, shoulders, and hips in a graceful, straight line (see page 12).
- Do your "shower" exercises regularly to keep your muscles at their normal feminine strength (see page 19).
- Adjust your chair to fit you perfectly (see page 16).
- Provide adequate task lighting (see page 43).
- Adjust the thermostat to suit you.

Emotional pain from boredom and frustration cause non-hunger eating.

✓ SOLUTIONS The solutions are simple:

- Make sure your regular meals and snacks are nourishing to your body, mind, and spirit.
- Allow enough time for the things you love about quiltmaking.
- Allow enough time for the steps of quiltmaking that are hard for you.
- Make only the quilts you want to make.
- Stretch yourself to learn new skills, but don't stretch too much on any one project.

Create a haven of emotional warmth for yourself while you are quilting:

- Put fresh flowers near your workstation.
- Put a picture of the person you are making the quilt for near your workstation.
- Put a piece of your very best work where you can see it.
- Tidy your immediate area.

Dining Out

Half of every food dollar is spent away from home. Retired quilters, quilters who work away from home, quilters who travel, and quilters who volunteer in their communities are all likely to eat away from home regularly.

The trick to maintaining your weight when dining out is deciding whether your meal is a celebration meal or whether it is an ordinary meal. Celebrations are days such as your birthday, Valentine's Day, Mother's Day, your wedding anniversary, Thanksgiving, Christmas, Hanukkah, and occasions commemorating accomplishments such as your graduation or promotion.

Celebrations: If it is a special occasion:
- Plan to eat modest portions of foods that hold special meaning for you.
- Order an appetizer and dessert.
- You do not have to consume your entire appetizer, entrée, or dessert. Eat the amount of each that is satisfying to you. Stop eating when you are full. Ask for a to-go container if you want to finish the food another day.

As a general guideline, eat in "celebration" mode on one day each month. Be cautious about feasting at someone else's celebration. If you must, eat modestly and plan low-fat and low-sugar meals for the rest of the day.

Ordinary Meals Away From Home: Non-celebration days are "regular" days. Your eating should mirror your regular meal plan.

Try these tips for weight-conscious restaurant dining:
- Drink a glass of water before you leave for the restaurant.
- If you feel very hungry, eat a packet of crackers with a glass of water. This will boost your blood sugar so you can make a good decision about what to order.
- If everyone in your party is ordering an appetizer, order fresh fruit or a salad with a squeeze of lemon juice.
- Order plenty of fresh fruits and vegetables with your entrée. Eat them first.
- Choose a lean entrée. A serving of meat is the size of a pack of cards. If you are served more meat than this, cut if off and ask for a to-go container.
- Avoid appetizers and desserts on non-celebration days

Fast Food: Fast food is loaded with fat. Most fast food is super-sized. The key to smart fast food eating is prior planning and moderation.

- The next time you drive through a fast food restaurant, ask for their nutritional information flyer. Study the flyer when you are not hungry. Highlight the entrées with calorie counts between 400-450 calories. If your favorite sandwich has more calories than this, note how much of it you will need to cut off and discard.
- Make a 3" x 5" card listing weight-conscious entrées and tape it inside your car's sun visor. If you travel, make a copy for your purse as well.
- Always consult your card before you order fast food. This is especially important when you are hungry.

Holiday Eating

The average American gains 7 pounds between Thanksgiving and New Year's Day. The holidays are a sugar-and-fat festival that tempt us to excess.

✓ SOLUTIONS

If you want to weigh the same on New Year's Day as you did on Thanksgiving morning, you must carefully balance your need for "feasting" on certain days of the season with sensible eating during the rest of the season.

Thanksgiving Day, Christmas Day, Hanukkah, and New Year's Eve are traditional days for feasting. It is very important to feast on these days. On these days, eat all of the foods that are special to you.

- Take modest portions of your favorite high-calorie foods.
- Take small bites, experiencing each one fully.
- After each bite, ask yourself if you are full. If so, stop eating. Do not allow anyone to pressure you to "clean your plate."

Holiday parties are another source of weight gain. Holiday parties call for careful meal planning if you wish to avoid weight gain:

- Choose very low-fat meals on the day of the party.
- Drink a big glass of water before you leave for the party.
- Make yourself a heaping plate of fresh fruits and vegetables at the party. Eat these before you have a single bite of "luxury food."
- Now return to the buffet and take modest portions of "luxury" foods. Take small bites and enjoy every single calorie. Stop eating when you are full.

Between-meal snacking is a big temptation during the holidays, especially at the office. If you want to partake of between-meal holiday treats:

- Plan meals that are low in fat and low in sugar to compensate for the calories in the treats.
- Weigh yourself on Thanksgiving morning and every day during the holidays. If you gain a pound, have a low-fat, no-sugar day with no treats. Check your scales the next morning to see if it is safe to resume eating treats.

Further Reading: Your library will have many titles on these subjects. Keywords include **health**, **nutrition**, **diet**, **junk food**, and **cookery**.

Better Get Moving!

14

Walking is a form of exercise that requires no new skills and no new equipment. It's a "come-as-you-are" lifetime fitness activity. Walking is the easiest, safest sport you can find. You can do it at any age. You can do it alone, with your family, or with good friends. Best of all, you get to set the pace.

- Women who walk lose more weight than women who jog.
- A 6-minute walk will flood your body with a sense of peace and contentment.
- A 6-minute walk will boost your metabolism by 15% and undo the metabolic slump caused by 50 minutes of quilting.

Walking provides these benefits:

- Immediate increase in energy
- Increased productivity while quilting
- Better sleep quality
- Slow, steady weight loss

A consistent walking program will restore your normal feminine muscles to their youthful robust state. You can restore your muscles even if you are ninety years old.

Walking has many other health benefits, it decreases the risk of:

- Heart disease
- Diabetes
- High cholesterol
- High blood pressure
- Cancer

Walking will benefit you as you get older, it:

- Prevents the bone loss of aging
- Increases agility and decreases your risk of hip fractures
- Improves arthritis everywhere in your body, even in your fingers
- Improves your memory

Walking will lengthen your life:

- Whether you are young, middle-aged, or elderly
- Whether you are in good health or suffer from obesity, heart disease, or cancer

Walking will have many positive effects on your emotions:

- Increased sense of well-being
- Increased self-confidence
- Increased resilience to stress
- Dramatic decline in depression

You can have all of the health benefits above if you walk for 90 minutes a week. Break up the 90 minutes any way you like:

- Nine 10-minute walks
- Three 30-minute walks
- Two 45-minute walks

To lose weight, you must walk 200 minutes a week. Break up those 200 minutes any way that fits into your schedule:

- A 10-minute walk before and after lunch on weekdays, plus a 20-minute walk after dinner each weekday
- A 15-minute walk before lunch each weekday, plus two 1-hour walks on the weekend (195 minutes)

The thought of walking so many minutes may sound overwhelming. Start with one 6-minute walk. Try it right now. Experience a rush of nature's feel-good chemicals. Strap on your watch and walk around the block. When 6 minutes are up, stop and close your eyes. You will feel a flood of peace and happiness surge through your body.

If you have small children, or if you are reading this in your nightclothes, walk inside your house. Walk for 6 minutes in a big circle through your dining room, kitchen, and family room, then stop, close your eyes, and feel a surge of peace and pleasure.

Your Walking Shoes

If you are taking a brief walk you can wear whatever is on your feet. Longer walks will be more comfortable if you wear socks to forestall blisters. Wear any comfortable shoes. If you own a pair of athletic shoes, wear those.

When you need a new pair of athletic shoes, choose a pair designed just for walking. A flexible shoe that bends with your foot is best. The thick, stiff sole of running shoes can cause fatigue on long walks.

Foot or Leg Problems

Ready-made "semi-orthotics" such as those made by Birkenstock® can help if you have foot problems. If you need more help than ready-mades can provide, your sports medicine doctor will prescribe custom inserts for you.

If leg cramps are a problem when you walk, see your family doctor for an evaluation. Sometimes the best treatment for this problem is building up your muscles by walking.

Long Walks or Short Walks?

The health benefits of short walks and long walks are the same, so you are free to select a walking program that fits into your schedule.

Long Walks

Double your pleasure on long walks by choosing a beautiful, uplifting route.

Morning is the best time for walking programs. Of people who begin a walking program:

- In the morning, 75% are still with it a year later
- During the day, 50% are still with it a year later
- In the evening, 25% are still at it a year later

Gail and Susan walk together for an hour every morning, they enjoy a pace that allows for conversation. Both lost 15 pounds last year.

Short Walks: "Take 10"

Take a 10-minute walk whenever you can. One quilter, an accountant, walks the halls of her office building for 10 minutes at mid-morning and mid-afternoon. At lunchtime she walks in the parking garage. She lost 25 pounds last year.

"Take 10" whenever you can:

- By parking at the far edge of the mall, then again when you return to your car
- While you watch soccer practice
- Around the pick-up circle at your child's school
- While your pasta is cooking
- During your hourly quilting break

THE BOTTOM LINE Just get moving. Walk when you can—you are going to be glad you did.

Bertha prefers short walks at a fast clip.

Getting Started

You can walk in your own neighborhood if:
- Your personal safety can be assured
- Dogs are not a problem
- Sidewalks are adequate

Walking Inside Your Home

Create a loop through your family room, kitchen, and dining room. Use it when it is icy, when you are a little "under the weather," or while the kids nap. Use it during your hourly 10-minute breaks from quiltmaking.

Walking at the Mall

Mall-walking is an increasingly popular activity. Malls open their doors to walkers early in the morning and late at night. Some malls offer walkers special tee shirts. Malls are perfect:
- In very cold weather
- In very hot weather
- For quilters with seasonal allergies
- For older quilters
- In bad weather for quilters who walk with a stroller

Outdoor Tracks

Outdoor jogging tracks are perfect for quilters who love fresh air. The grassy center makes a perfect play area for your kids. You and your kids will be able to see each other at all times.

Bicycle and Jogging Trails

These trails provide a safe, beautiful environment for a walk during daylight hours. They are perfect for almost any quilter, whether she walks alone, with a friend, or with children in a stroller.

How to Begin Your Walking Program

A slow, gentle start is your best recipe for success.
- Start slow. Take three 10-minute walks the first week.
- Walk at a regular time, if you can.
- Walk loops at first, so you can return home when you become tired.
- Have a written bad-weather backup plan: the mall, a stationary bike, or a loop inside your home.

About Dogs

In four thousand miles of walking, I've had only one ugly confrontation with a dog.

- Most dogs will respond to friendly, quiet patter. Face the dog and say, "Hello, I'm your neighbor. I'm glad to see you. It's OK, I'm just out walking. You are a beautiful dog, etc." Continue to talk in a friendly voice until the dog relaxes.

Maximizing Your Chances for Success

There are a few things you can do to help ensure the success of your walking program.

- Start slow and build up to the amount of time you have chosen as your goal.
- Find the pace that is most pleasurable for you. Your personal pace may be strolling, ambling, plodding, meandering, moseying, rambling, or shuffling along. Slow walkers lose more body fat than joggers.
- Take joy and pleasure in your surroundings as you walk.
- Pause for one minute at the end of your walk and enjoy the sense of well-being.

Endorphins

Endorphins are natural brain chemicals that are produced anytime we exercise for 6 minutes or more. Endorphins:

- Are natural painkillers 200 times stronger than the drug morphine. They are natural, non-addictive tranquilizers and mood-elevators.
- Cause feelings of well-being. In times of pain or stress they can even cause euphoria.
- Enhance performance on endurance tasks such as quiltmaking.

If you are a new walker you will experience an endorphin rush when you have walked 6 minutes or about two blocks. You will probably have to pause and close your eyes to feel it at first. You will experience it again when you stop walking.

Experienced walkers feel the endorphin rush by their second stride and continue to feel the rush for 30 minutes after their walks.

The rush is a perfect pick-me-up on long drives to quilt shows. Walk for 6 minutes at rest stops and gas stations.

Water

Drinking water before and after your walk can help you succeed in losing weight. Drinking water:

- Opens up your fat deposits so they are available for fat burning
- Allows your body to complete the chemical reaction that burns fat
- Fights tension and fatigue, which allows you to walk longer

Wheelchairs

If you are in a wheelchair, you can burn 150 calories by wheeling yourself around for 30 minutes. You can expect all of the health benefits, previously listed, from wheeling.

Other Fitness Activities

Walking is the safest sport. It requires no new motor skills and no new equipment. Some quilters may prefer another fitness activity. The following also have a low risk of injury:

- Stationary bicycling
- Swimming
- Bicycling
- Cross-country skiing

Moderate-risk activities include:

- Jogging
- Dancing

Further Reading: Your library will have many references on this topic. Check these keywords: **walking, fitness walking, exercise**, and **physical fitness.**

THE QUILTERS IN THIS CHAPTER

Gayle Sanford (page 95) has been quilting for 20 years. She is the mother of two grown sons and works for the constable of Richardson, Texas.

Susan Sembera (page 95) has been a quilter for 10 years. She is the mother of two college-age children and works as an accountant.

Bertha Mallard (page 95) has been a quilter for three years. She is the mother of a grown son and the grandmother of one. She is retired after 30 years of Federal Service.

Stephanie has adjusted her chair so that her knees make a right angle. She adjusted her sewing table so that her wrists remain straight when she sews.

Workshops, Shows & Workspaces

15 Workshops, Retreats & Shows

Workshops

A quilt workshop provides close contact with a compassionate and inspiring teacher who shares her unique vision and innovative quiltmaking techniques. The learning that happens in every quilt workshop helps you to dream your own dreams and to bring those dreams into tangible reality.

A few simple measures can assure you of a workshop experience that will nourish your body, mind, and soul. Careful planning can help to assure your physical and emotional comfort during your quiltmaking workshop.

Supplies

Study the supply list for the workshop. In addition to the supplies specified by your teacher, put together a "workshop kit" containing the following: writing and marking supplies, hand sewing supplies, machine sewing supplies, rotary cutting supplies, and ironing supplies. If you are over 45, plan to bring a goose-neck lamp or other task light to help you to see during the workshop. Bring extension cords for all your appliances, including a heavy-duty cord for your iron. Pack a grounded three-outlet tap to allow you to plug three appliances into one outlet. Label all of your equipment with your name.

Seating

If you are petite, short-waisted, or have back problems, you can use inexpensive pillow forms to customize a standard folding chair to fit you perfectly.

PETITE QUILTERS AND SHORT-WAISTED QUILTERS If you are shorter than 5' 3" your feet will not be able to rest flat on the floor when you sit in a standard folding chair. This means your feet cannot help stabilize your hips and upper body. This leads to back strain. Solve this problem by placing a 12" square pillow on the floor for your feet. Your feet can rest flat on the pillow and support your hips and upper body.

If you are petite or short-waisted, the backs of folding chairs will jab into your mid-back. You can obtain the upper back support you need by attaching a 12" x 15" pillow to the back of your folding chair with an 18" bungee cord.

Place the pillow vertically. Affix it so the center of the pillow presses into the small of your back.

QUILTERS WITH BACK PROBLEMS Use an 18" bungee cord to attach a 12" x 15" pillow to the back of your folding chair. The vertical pillow will provide support for your entire upper body and take strain off your lower back. Don't forget to keep your feet flat on the floor to stabilize your hips. Later, you can cover the pillow forms with washable cases that express your unique creative vision.

Clothing and Shoes

Much of your comfort at the workshop will depend on the garments and footwear you select.

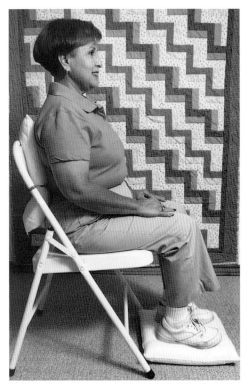

Estela, who is 4'10", uses two standard pillow forms to customize a folding chair to fit.

CLOTHING Choose a comfortable outfit with ample wearing ease at the waist and shoulders. This is important because your waist size will increase when you sit. It will also increase as the day goes on. Wearing ease at the shoulder will allow you to work easily at the machine, ironing board, and cutting mat.

SHOES If you will be standing quite a bit to iron and rotary cut, wear your athletic shoes. If you will be sitting all day, choose comfortable slip-on shoes with good arch support. Your feet will be working hard to stabilize your hips and upper body.

Loading Your Car

When you load your supplies into your car, be sure to keep your back straight and knees bent; lift heavy items by straightening your knees. See page 11 for detailed instructions on lifting heavy objects safely.

Personality Type

Plan your level of participation in the workshop according to your natural personality type.

- **Extroverts:** If you are an outgoing person, you will be energized by the excitement of the workshop. Your creative juices will flow freely. Extroverts will design, cut, and sew during the workshop.
- **Introverts:** If you are a quiet, inward person, you may feel overwhelmed by the commotion of the workshop. Pack supplies for the workshop, but feel free to simply observe and absorb. You may want to walk around quietly and see what others are doing. You can try the new techniques once you are back home.

Enjoying the Journey

Plan to enjoy the drive to the workshop.

- Keep a lumbar cushion in your car, if you need one. Position it above your buttocks, to fit into the curve of your back.
- Wear comfortable slip-on shoes with good arch support for the drive.
- Drink 8 ounces of water each hour you travel. The fluid will lubricate your eyes and the joints of your hands, wrists, and back. If you drink water, you won't have any trouble remembering to stop for a break every hour.
- Maintain good posture while you drive.
- Stretch and do your "shower" exercises when you stop every hour. This will erase tension from your body and begin to heal any damage to your joints and muscles caused by the drive.
- If traffic or fatigue send your shoulders up toward your ears, do "Maybe-Sos" while you are driving, if you can do so safely.
- As you travel, eat healthful nutritious foods. Focus on fruits, vegetables, low-fat protein sources, and juices. Avoid beverages containing sugar or caffeine. If you become drowsy, use strongly flavored snacks to wake you up, such as raspberry-flavored yogurt, or peanuts flavored with hot peppers.
- Make sure you have clear directions or know the route. If you don't know the route, travel with someone who can help you navigate.

At the Workshop

To minimize stress and maximize health:

- Plan to arrive a few minutes early so that unloading and workstation selection are peaceful and enjoyable.
- When unloading your supplies, bend your knees, keep your back straight, and lift heavy items by straightening your bent knees. Reverse the process to put them down.

- Select a spot for your workstation that will put you at your preferred distance from the instructor. Place your chair cushions on your folding chair. Set up your machine and task lighting.
- Maintain good posture throughout the workshop. Keep your feet flat on the floor. Tuck in your tummy and chin. Maintain a straight line between your hips, shoulders, and ears. Keep your shoulders low and back.
- Take rest and stretch breaks regularly. If the teacher does not break every hour, move quietly to the back of the room and stretch. To help unkink your postural muscles, sway back and forth as if you were rocking a baby.

Retreats

Surely heaven is like a quilt retreat. No phones. Unlimited time to devote to quiltmaking. The company of other quilters. Food, lovingly prepared by friends. And laughter. A quilt retreat is the world's best recipe for restoration of your body, mind, and soul.

Before You Go

Review the section above for tips on packing for and driving to a workshop. In addition to the above, if you have established a healthy eating plan, talk to the retreat chairwoman and find out what will be served at meals. If your meal plan differs substantially, bring some of your own food, including snacks.

During the Retreat

Attention to a few things during the retreat will assure that you come home healthier than you were when you left.
- Maintain good posture throughout the retreat.
- Be sure the seating fits you. This is especially important if you tend to "binge quilt" at retreats. Bring cushions to custom-fit folding chairs to your body, or bring the "secretarial chair" from your sewing room. The condition of your back will dictate how serious you need to be about this.
- Take a 10-minute break every hour. Breaks are very important when you "binge quilt." Stretch. Take a walk through the grounds of the retreat center. Take a nap.
- Your eyes need a 30-second break every 5 minutes. Lift your head and look out the window for a few moments.
- Vary your tasks during the day. If you do, your body will feel better when you get back home.

- Take Tylenol for minor aches and pains caused by "binge quilting." Non-steroidal anti-inflammatory agents can promote microscopic scarring in your muscles and tendons.
- Take a multivitamin with minerals every day while on retreat. It will help your eyes, skin, fingers, and back.
- Drink a glass of water every hour. This will lubricate your eyes and joints. This is very important in binge quilting situations. The water will also decrease your appetite and allow your metabolism to rev up during your breaks.

Introverts at Retreats

If you are a quiet, inward person, the commotion of the retreat may inhibit your creativity. Don't plan on doing much design work at the retreat. Instead, plan to:
- Hand or machine piece previously cut patches
- Appliqué previously prepared fabrics
- Hand quilt a previously marked quilt
- Sew the binding on a quilt
- Find quiet corners for conversation
- Take long walks
- Take naps
- If you want to, go to bed at your regular time.

Quilt Shows

Attending a quilt show is the best way to recharge your quilting battery. Seeing the best work of other quiltmakers will inspire and challenge you. Visiting the vendor area puts new fabrics and tools within your reach. A quilt show will leave you energized and excited about getting back home to quilt. To maximize the benefits of attending:
- Choose comfortable clothing with plenty of wearing ease at the shoulder and waist.
- Select soft-soled shoes with good arch support. You will be on your feet most of the day.
- Keep your head, shoulders, hips, and ankles in a graceful straight line.
- Take breaks. Set your watch to beep on the hour. Mark your location on your program and take a 10-minute break to stretch, to visit the rest room, and to drink 8 ounces of water. Sit down for a few minutes and relax. Check your feet for swelling and re-lace your shoes more loosely, if needed.

- If you are using a backpack, shift its position frequently from right shoulder to left, from your back to your front.
- Rolling bags are another good choice for carrying your purchases. Choose one with a handle that does not force you to bend over.
- Choosing foods and beverages with supreme nutrients will assure you of maximum pleasure, energy, and inspiration at the show. Don't waste 30 minutes in line waiting to buy high-fat, high-salt, high-sugar, high-chemical-additive meals. Take 10 minutes at home to pack a lunch. Carry it in your backpack. Bring fruit juices in individual servings, bottled water, and a high-protein, low-fat lunch and snacks. Choose a seat near the lunch line and study the details on the quilted garments that parade by while you eat your healthy, energizing lunch.

Estela has chosen loose, comfortable clothing for her trip to a quilt show. She is wearing athletic shoes with good arch support.

SUMMARY: The secrets of maximizing the benefits of workshops, retreats, and shows are these:
- Maintain good posture
- Bring cushions to make sure your seat will fit you
- Choose comfortable clothing with ample wearing ease
- Select footwear that will minimize foot pain
- Take a break every hour
- Pack healthful and nutritious foods and beverages

16 Design a Workspace to Fit Your Body

Your workspace can be a place for a vacation from the cares and worries of your life. A place to be comforted, warmed, and soothed. A place to dream your own dreams. A place to create quilts that give tangible form to those dreams. It can be a place for healing your body, your mind, and your soul.

A well-designed workspace will buy you:

- A comfortable and pain-free back
- A lessened chance of developing carpal tunnel syndrome
- Increased enjoyment of the quiltmaking process
- Decreased errors
- A productivity increase of 25% every year

In order to be sure the health of your body, mind, and soul improves while you work:

- Make sure you have adequate lighting
- Place all of the equipment in your sewing room at the correct height for your body

Worktable

Your work surface should be four inches below the height of your bent elbow. One way to obtain a worktable that is the right height for you is to buy a folding "cafeteria" table at an office supply store. These cost about $30. Boost the table to the proper height with lengths of white PVC pipe.

You will probably prefer a slightly lower table height for rotary cutting. Some quilters obtain the best of both worlds by keeping a pair of thick-soled clogs under their worktables. They slip the clogs on when they rotary cut.

Sewing Machine

Most sewing machine tables are several inches too high for good forearm and wrist health. When you are sitting with your feet flat on the floor and your knees and elbows are bent at 90°, your fingertips should rest lightly on the throat plate of your machine. See Chapter 3 (page 26) for more on this.

The adjustable Table-mate®, available in many home furnishings catalogs, is one good choice for a sewing machine table. Its backward-C-shaped supports allow you to swivel when you get up to press a seam. One is shown in the photo on page 99. Office superstores sell adjustable computer tables.

You can also shorten the legs of an old table so it fits you. See page 29 for more about this.

Avoid tilting sewing machine platforms if you have carpal tunnel syndrome or another repetitive strain injury. These platforms force you to bend your wrists when you sew and may worsen your injury.

If you wear a cervical collar for neck problems, talk to your doctor about wearing it when you sew at your machine. The collar will assure you of good head posture.

Ironing Board

A simple calculation will help you find the correct height for your ironing board. Measure the height that will allow your elbow to be bent at a 90° angle while you iron. Subtract 4" from that. This will be the correct height for your ironing board. See an ironing board adjusted to fit Stephanie on page 10.

If your board will not rise up to the height you need, turn it over and study the hardware that adjusts its height. Some ironing boards can be modified to be taller if you drill away the "stops" that limit their extension. If your board cannot be adjusted further, you can devise a platform to lift it higher or buy an ironing board that will adjust to the correct height.

Seating

If you spend more than one hour a week on quiltmaking, you must invest in seating that fits you perfectly. Chapter 1 covers this in detail. Briefly, your quilt-making chair should allow your feet to rest flat on the floor and have an adjustable backrest to support your lumbar spine.

If your dining chairs are the correct height for you, you can fix a small cushion to a chair back with an 18" bungee cord. Position the cushion to fit into your lumbar spine area. You must place the cushion high enough so you can move your buttocks to the rear of the seat. See page 7 to see how Stephanie positions her lumbar cushion in a chair.

Long-Arm Quilting Machines

Adjust the height of your machine so you can keep your elbows bent at 90° when you grasp the handles. Keep your back and neck straight while you work. See page 12 for a photo of Stephanie at her long-arm machine. Her machine is adjusted to the correct height and she is in perfect posture.

It is important to remain loose and relaxed when you use your long-arm machine. If you are tensing up or craning your neck forward, you may not have enough light. Invest in two halogen torchlights. If you use a cervical collar, ask your doctor if you should wear it when you use your machine.

You will be on your feet for long hours when you quilt with your long-arm machine. Wear a pair of shoes with good arch support when you work. When you need a new pair, choose a pair of walking shoes or a pair of aerobic shoes. They have flexible soles and will allow you to move around easily.

Lighting

Good lighting is always a better solution than a stronger eyeglass prescription. Provide bright, glare-free light at each of your workstations. Your goal is to have noonday brightness wherever you are working. Choose one or more of the following:

- Halogen torchlights provide bright, indirect light. Find them at office superstores for about $15 apiece. A pair will light any workspace.
- Incandescent task lights: a hinged lamp over your machine and twin hinged lamps over your cutting table. Sewing catalogs and office superstores carry these.
- Fluorescent Ott® task lights. These provide light similar to daylight. Quilters love them because color looks the same at night as it does by daylight. They are expensive. Find these in sewing catalogs and quilt shops.
- Fluorescent ceiling fixtures fitted with four to eight 5000 degree Kelvin bulbs. The bulbs cost about $7.00 apiece, a significant savings over the Ott lights. Find them at lighting stores.

Storage

Keep heavy equipment such as your sewing machine or serger stored close at hand so you do not have to lift them while they are at an arm's length. Store lightweight tools, such as your rotary cutting ruler, farther away.

Further Reading: Your library may have books with more information. Use these keywords to begin your search: **ergonomics, human factors engineering, occupational health, office layout, workplace, lighting, carpal tunnel syndrome, repetitive strain injury,** and **cervical neck disease**.

Acknowledgments and Thanks

This book is the product of ten years of study and work. It could never have come about without the encouragement and support of Sandra Hatch, editor of *Quilt World*. In 1988, Sandra reviewed some material I'd written and invited me to write a column for her magazine.

Thanks are also due to the wonderful readers of *Quilt World* who shared their stories and their solutions. This book is a response to their request for "more."

A word of grateful acknowledgment goes to the staff of C&T Publishing who believed in this book, especially Annie Nelson, Diane Pedersen, Trish Katz, and Sara MacFarland.

I am indebted to my husband, Arnie, and to our daughter, Sarah, for their patience and support. I owe my love of learning to the four generations of women in my family who used the Library of Congress as their personal library and to my parents who never stopped learning. My sister, Mary, and my god-mother, Pigeon, have always encouraged me.

I am lucky to have so many talented and compassionate quilting friends. Without their support this book would not be. I especially thank Janet Cestaro, Margaret Noah, Susan Wilson, Jennifer Lokey, Nancy Wells, Mary MacInnis, and the members of my small group, The Batty Quilters. I also thank my friends JoAnn Stephens, Vickie Mower, Barbara Kelton, Debra Copley, Laurie Rickard, Janet Fein, Linda Smith, and Bill Simpson.

I am deeply grateful to my brother and Irish twin, Stephen C. Delaney, who took the photos for this book. Finally, I would like to thank the quilters who appear in the book, Stephanie Tallent, Bertha Mallard, Elizabeth Murray, Elise SansSouci, Jan Gadberry, Betty Lou Wood, Susan Sembera, Gayle Stanford, Ginny Kenney, Debbie Campbell, Julie Flemming, and Estela Dela Fuente.

Author's Note: I welcome your comments, tips, and questions. I will incorporate them into future columns, articles, and into the next edition of this book. Write to me at 4100 W. 15th Street, Suite 220, Plano, Texas, 75093, or at susandelaneymech@airmail.net. I regret that I cannot answer every letter personally.

Index

Glossary

disc (intervertebral disc)—a ring of cartilage and fibers with a gelatinous center, located between the vertebrae

ergonomics—the science of making tools and workstations to fit the body of the worker

lens—a clear structure in the eye resembling a camera's lens. It focuses images on the retina

ligaments—strong bands of body tissue that keep bones from shifting too far out of place

macula—a small area of densely packed light-sensing cells in the retina

retina—the area in the back of the eyeball which contains light-sensitive cells

tendons—strong cords of body tissue that attach muscles to bone

vertebrae—the bones that make up the spine

Recommended Reading

Barbach, Lonnie. *The Pause: Positive Approaches to Menopause.* Signet Health, New York: Dutton, 1993.

Bean, Constance. *The Better Back Book.* New York: Wm. Morrow, 1989.

Eisenberg, Arlene, Sandee Hathaway, Heidi Murkoff. *What to Expect When You Are Expecting.* New York: Workman Publishing, 1991.

Peel, Kathy. *The Family Manager's Everyday Survival Guide.* New York: Ballantine Books, 1998.

Roesch, Roberta. *Time Management for Busy People.* New York: McGraw Hill, 1998.

Pascarelli, MD, Emil, Deborah Quilter. *Repetitive Strain Injury: A Computer User's Guide.* New York: John Wiley & Sons, Inc., 1994.

Time-Life Books. *The Fit Back.* Alexandria, VA: Morristown, NJ: 1988.

Williams, Dr. Mark. *The American Geriatric Society's Complete Guide to Aging and Health.* New York: Harmony, 1995.

Sources

Clotilde
Box 3000
Louisiana, MO
63353-3000
(800) 772-2891
www.clotilde.com
vision aids tested by
sewers

The Lighthouse
36-20 Northern
Boulevard
Long Island City, NY
11101
(800) 829-0500
www.lighthouse.org
low-vision aids

Maxi Aids
P.O.Box 3209
Farmingdale, NY 11735
(800) 522-6294
www.maxiaids.com
aids for low vision and
other disabilities

Other Fine Books From C&T Publishing:

An Amish Adventure: 2nd Edition, Roberta Horton

The Art of Classic Quiltmaking, Harriet Hargrave & Sharyn Craig

The Art of Silk Ribbon Embroidery, Judith Baker Montano

Elegant Stitches, Judith Baker Montano

Exploring Machine Trapunto: New Dimensions, Hari Walner

Fancy Appliqué: 12 Lessons to Enhance Your Skills, Elly Sienkiewicz

Fabric Shopping with Alex Anderson, Alex Anderson

Fantastic Fabric Folding: Innovative Quilting Projects, Rebecca Wat

Free Stuff for Collectors on the Internet, Judy Heim and Gloria Hansen

Free Stuff for Quilters on the Internet, 2nd Ed. Judy Heim and Gloria Hansen

Free Stuff for Gardeners on the Internet, Judy Heim and Gloria Hansen

From Fiber to Fabric: The Essential Guide to Quiltmaking Textiles, Harriet Hargrave

Hand Quilting with Alex Anderson: Six Projects for Hand Quilters, Alex Anderson

Jacobean Rhapsodies: Composing with 28 Appliqué Designs, Patricia B. Campbell
    and Mimi Ayars

Mastering Quilt Marking, Pepper Cory

Pieced Roman Shades, Terrell Sundermann

Quilt It for Kids, Pam Bono

Quilts for Fabric Lovers, Alex Anderson

Quilts from Europe: Projects and Inspiration, Gül Laporte

Shadow Quilts: Easy to Design Multiple Image Quilts, Donna Slusser
    and Patricia Margaret

Six Color World: Color, Cloth, Quilts & Wearables, Yvonne Porcella

Skydyes: A Visual Guide to Fabric Painting, Mickey Lawler

Start Quilting with Alex Anderson: Six Projects for First-Time Quilters, Alex Anderson

Through the Garden Gate: Quilters and Their Gardens, Jean and Valori Wells

Wild Birds: Designs for Appliqué & Quilting, Carol Armstrong

Yvonne Porcella: Art & Inspirations, Yvonne Porcella

For more information write for a free catalog:
C&T Publishing, Inc.
P.O. Box 1456
Lafayette, CA 94549
(800) 284-1114
http://www.ctpub.com
e-mail: ctinfo@ctpub.com

For quilting supplies:
Cotton Patch Mail Order
3405 Hall Lane, Dept. CTB
Lafayette, CA 94549
(800) 835-4418
(925) 283-7883
e-mail: quiltusa@yahoo.com
Web: www.quiltusa.com